The Party Goes On

THE PARTY GOES ON

The Persistence of
the Two-Party System in
the United States

XANDRA KAYDEN

EDDIE MAHE, JR.

Basic Books, Inc., Publishers   New York

Library of Congress Cataloging-in-Publication Data

Kayden, Xandra.
   The party goes on.

   Bibliographical notes: p. 221.
   Includes index.
   1. Political parties—United States—History.
2. Democratic Party—History. 3. Republican Party
—History. I. Mahe, Eddie, 1936–   II. Title.
JK2261.K39   1985   324.273'09   85–47557
ISBN   0–465–05453–6

Contents

PART IV

CONCLUSION   *181*

Acknowledgments

THE AUTHORS wish to thank the Institute of Politics, Harvard University for its support of this project from the very beginning, for receiving the grant from the Earhart Foundation enabling Xandra Kayden to devote full time to the book, and for providing an invaluable opportunity for Dr. Kayden to meet and talk with people involved in the parties and campaigns throughout the fall of 1984 at the biweekly Institute suppers for study group leaders and their guests. Jonathan Moore, director of the Institute, and Mary McTighe, Jocelyn Moore, Andrew Robertson, and Sonia Wallenberg, and the rest of the staff and fellows were particularly helpful. Others who played a significant role in getting the book off the ground were Arthur Singer, the Earhart Foundation, Robert Ducas, and Martin Kessler at Basic Books. Those who helpfully read chapters or provided critical material include: Marc Braden, Kent Cooper, Robert J. Keefe, Michael J. Malbin, Don Nathan, William Schneider, and Rick Stearns. The staff of Market Opinion Research was also helpful. James Q. Wilson read the entire manuscript in every draft. Xandra Kayden wrote the book and Eddie Mahe, Jr., participated in discussions of drafts of the chapters. His associate, LaDonna Lee, and the rest of his staff also provided material and support.

PART
I

THE DISMAL STATE
OF THE PARTIES

1

Introduction

IN 1972, David Broder, one of the nation's leading political journalists, published a book entitled *The Party's Over.* [1] His theme echoed the beliefs of many political observers in the press, in the academic community, and in the world at large that the American two-party system—arguably the oldest party system in the world —was in serious danger of collapse. Although he was pessimistic about the situation, Broder was by no means writing about a certainty: "If we engage ourselves in politics, and particularly concern ourselves with the workings of those strangely neglected institutions, the political parties . . . we may find the instrument of national self-renewal in our hands." [2] Broder's theme of decline was picked up like a banner and carried throughout the 1970s and well into the 1980s as an obituary of a curious institution, which we had viewed alternately with affection and disgust. The death of the parties became the premise of most analyses thereafter.

This book is about political rebirth. The American party system, like the Phoenix, has risen from the ashes of turmoil a half generation ago. The current system is not the same as it was before. It is a new animal, dependent on different resources, performing different tasks. It is based in Washington and draws its strength from small contributors across the nation. It is a professional organization that provides more resources to campaigns than any other single participant in the electoral process. No individual, no group can compete with the party's ability to raise and spend money, and to provide a host of other services from polling information to press releases.

The modern party is coming to play a greater role in the selection of its nominees—although the presidency itself remains largely outside its influence because of the sheer number of primaries and caucuses. It is also becoming more influential in public policy, indirectly through its role in candidate selection and the help it gives in issue research during the course of a campaign, and directly through its own efforts such as media advertising to influence the behavior of elected officials.

What is different about the party—beside the amount of money it is able to raise—is the way the money flows. The national party used to exist solely for the purpose of selecting the national nominee and was financed by the state parties, but now it provides the money (and not infrequently the candidates) to the states. Where there is an active county organization, it, too, is often dependent on the funds and programs eminating from the top. But the local parties, which were populated by volunteers, no longer play a strong role in American politics. There are many reasons for the decline of grassroot politics, but its disappearance suggests that the myths we hold about our political institutions need revision.

Throughout the book, with the exception of chapter 6 on the voters, our analysis is based on party structure: the organization itself which is made up of relatively small numbers of people who raise the funds, work with candidates, argue over policy positions, and sometimes go on to elective office themselves. Although most party workers in America are volunteers, those we are writing about are the paid professionals, who make up the core group and have the technical ability to develop the programs, write the letters, and make the appeals responsible for the party building that has taken place in the last ten years. It is this group that is able to reach out to a much larger constituency of party identifiers in the population to raise extraordinary amounts of money and make everything else possible. It is this group, we believe, that will change the nature of politics and partisanship in the United States for the rest of this century.

The people who work for the two national major parties represent a generational change in American politics. They bring to their jobs a new set of values and expectations. The sense of professionalism among them is strong, as is their confidence in their ability to turn the party organizations into more than they have ever been before. They are not as ideological as many of the active partisans who support them in the hinterlands, but they have the capacity to reach out to increasing numbers of our citizenry and instill among them a new feeling about the parties and a new feeling about all of our institutions. Whether it is done with computers, charismatic leadership, or mirrors, the net result is growing partisan identification, particularly in the Republican party.

The Democratic and Republican parties are not equal in strength, but they are not entirely unbalanced in electoral competition. We believe the GOP is the prototype of the modern party and that the Democrats will catch up. We also believe that both parties have gone through a remarkable rebuilding process since Broder's book first appeared and have learned a lot from each other. The national committees of both parties are more like each other today than they are like their predecessors ten, and certainly twenty, years ago.

Political Parties: What Are They?

Political scientists have had a hard time defining parties because they perform very different functions in different sorts of governments. They are both organizations and processes, and sometimes they are part of the fabric of identity for individuals, groups, and ideas. In a parliamentary system, a party has a clearer path to governance than a party in a system of separated powers such as ours. A party in a communist country does not contest elections, but does legitimate the regime in power. All parties appear to serve as a mechanism for integrating citizens into government.

Most analysts agree that parties are structured groups; usually, but not always, large groups representing some division in the society.[3] Parties always seek power. The eighteenth-century British political philosopher and statesman, Edmund Burke, developed one of the first positive definitions when he described a party as a "body of men united for promoting by their joint endeavors the national interest upon some particular principle in which they are all agreed."[4] E. E. Schattschneider, a mid-twentieth century political scientist, thought of a party more simply in terms of its purpose and the methods it used to attain its purpose. If its object is power, the control of government, the method of obtaining control in a democracy is election.[5] To many political scientists writing today, contesting elections is *the* function of parties in America.

If one thinks about party systems, instead of parties per se, there are two broad conceptions we often use (which are somewhat antithetical) in describing our two-party structure. There is the pluralist model developed originally by James Madison, and a more "holistic" model developed by noted political scientist Walter Dean Burnham.

In the more traditional pluralist view, American politics is based on unstable, but nonetheless legitimate and often-enduring, coalitions of groups that align themselves with the parties and seek to win office accordingly. The "out" party becomes an umbrella for the disaffected of the "in" party. Shifts in partisanship and who wins office are based on the assumption that neither party will move too far from the center because the choice then would require a drastic change in government policy and behavior.

To Burnham, on the other hand, the parties "are not action instrumentalities of definable and broad social collectivities; as organizations they are, consequently, interested in control of offices but not of government in the broader sense. . . . It follows from this that once successful routines are established or reestablished for winning office, there is no motivation among party leaders to disrupt the routines of the game." What changes the game, according

to Burnham, is "the application of overwhelming external force."[6]
This explains the phenomenon of party decline and realignment:

> The periodic rhythm of American electoral politics, the cycle of oscilla-
> tion between the normal and the disruptive corresponds precisely to the
> existence of largely unfettered developmental change in the socioeco-
> nomic system and its absence in the country's political institutions.
> ... The socioeconomic system develops but the institutions of electoral
> politics and policy formation remain essentially unchanged. Moreover,
> they do not have much capacity to adjust incrementally to demand
> arising from socioeconomic dislocations. Dysfunctions centrally related
> to this process become more and more visible, until finally entire classes,
> regions, or other major sectors of the population are directly injured or
> come to see themselves as threatened by imminent danger. The trigger-
> ing event occurs, critical realignments follow, and the universe of policy
> and of electoral coalitions is broadly redefined. ... It is as symptomatic
> of political nonevolution in this country as are the archaic and increas-
> ingly rudimentary structures of the political parties themselves. But
> even more importantly, critical realignment may well be defined as the
> chief tension-management device available to so peculiar a political
> system.[7]

Society changes; the political system is too rigid and un-
developed to respond accordingly, so the pressure rises to a point
which forces a realignment. In the process, interest groups, particularly those of a moralistic nature, emerge and wield considerable
influence. Every election in the past decade has brought with it
analyses as to whether or not this was the long-awaited realigning
election. At this writing at least, 1984 appears to be the most likely
candidate, but only after 1988 will we know with certainty.

The view that parties are purely mechanisms for winning elections appears to be more a description than a definition. Burnham
took a larger view, but he held immutable the party structure, and
we would argue that it is precisely the party structure that has
changed. And if this is the case, there must be more to what the
parties do than political scientists, at least, have been willing to
credit them with in the past few years.

It is our view that the parties exist principally for the purpose
of influencing public policy (leaning more to Madison), and that

in order to attain that end, strong parties must have control over their nominations for elective office and the resources needed to contest elections. We believe that strong parties are characterized by a meaningful organizational structure: one that can make decisions and one that is relatively accessible to those who seek to participate in public events. If the parties can make decisions, they are in a better position to respond to emerging interests and do not necessarily have to behave as passively as Burnham suggests. Party managers can be more like architects designing a canal than river bottoms over which the water flows. If they can manage the interests, the parties are in the best position to build coalitions for governance, to effect compromise, and to promote consensus.

Whether or not the parties achieve their potential, they are the infrastructure of American political life and are not likely to disappear. In fact, it is unlikely that a new party will replace one of the existing two major parties unless we are all but overcome by cataclysmic changes. Weak as they have been in controlling any of the functions we would propose for them, they are legally bound to us because of their almost-monopolistic control of ballot access, and because we structure our legislatures according to party allegiance. Independent candidates and third parties complain at every election that the system is unfair to them. They are right. The system has been designed for the benefit of the major parties and most of us would not want it any other way.

The political parties are more than the sum of their parts. They represent the significant socioeconomic cleavages in the nation, and they embody within them the aspirations we hold for ourselves and our society. They are both the practical application of political philosophies or how the world ought to function, and they are the mix of special interests, which lay claim to a share in the distribution of public goods and services. The parties frame the political consciousness of most citizens; certainly they frame the political debate. All of these functions add up to attitudes and ideas, but the parties are more than that: they are also organizations with active members. Our thesis is that the parties function at their best when the organizational part of their character is strong, and that the organization is growing stronger.

How We Got to Where We Were:
The Nadir of the Parties

In politics it is always hard to know if one is in the eye of a hurricane or whether the storm has passed. At the risk of jumping to conclusions, it does appear now, in the mid-1980s, that the turbulent times of the past few decades are over. As optimistic as we might sound today, clearly there was cause for the popular prejudice that the parties were in bad straits. Although we have never been very trusting when it comes to the parties, they fell on particularly hard times in the early part of this century during the Progressive Era, which stripped them of much of their internal power (via primaries, nonpartisan election, elimination of the party ballot, and so forth). By the time the New Deal was past, partisan loyalties were high because of the dramatic shift in the role of government, but party organization was weak. It was in that condition that we drifted into the 1950s, when scholars began to do the massive studies of political behavior we now take for granted as marking the temperature of our political system.

By the 1960s, new generations had grown up without the experience of partisan loyalties their elders had. The combination of little sustaining loyalty and weak organization made it difficult for the parties to move to adopt new issues, or effectively halt the growing ideological polarization. The parties became a battleground for the interests. They could not bring the new interests in and force compromise; they could not create consensus. Those on the extremes accused the parties of being too representative of the status quo, and those in the middle thought the parties, along with all the other major institutions of our society, were just too weak to mean very much at all to anyone. We had entered an era of alienation. Presidential primaries brought national candidates to the party who failed to represent the mainstream of that party's membership. Everyone felt locked out and few felt there was much in the parties worth fighting for in the first place. Brilliant leadership might have made a difference, but it was unlikely such leadership would be found in as massive a body as the party; it came more easily to light in the Senate and other places where television cameras could focus.

In the 1970s, things reached a new low, but they began to turn around. The Democratic party was deeply in debt and had taken many years to retire the debt of the Humphrey campaign of 1968. The Republican party was subordinated to the White House even more than usual in the presidential re-election bid of Richard Nixon, to the point where it was ordered out of any challenge to thirty-three Democratic incumbent congressional races. Watergate not only tainted the party image, it also cost it a number of its professional consultants.

By the time we reached the 1980s, several new crises had arisen, due in large measure to the campaign finance reform legislation passed in the 1970s and the political after-effects of two decades of disillusionment. To many, these latest problems were nails in the coffin.

- Interests had come to dominate campaign spending, and the new phenomenon of independent spending (a favorite of the New Right groups) was going to sweep America into an ideological fervor and political chaos, threatening the very survival of both parties;
- The national Republican party was strong and extraordinarily wealthy, and the Democrats would never be able to catch up. It would be the end of the two-party system we had known for more than a century.
- The centralization of the party system, without effective intermediary structures, was threatening the nature of democracy. "Back to the grassroots!" was the cry heard everywhere from candidates for party chairpersons to very sage and respected political scientists.

It is our contention that all of these things might have happened, but they did not. Instead, we believe, both parties went through a metamorphosis and are now emerging in a far stronger organizational position than they have ever been. The Democratic reforms, however colorfully brought about, recognized the need for a new basis for participation in politics. The Republican money, and the restraints the law imposed on potential large donors, put the party back into the business of controlling the nomination and, in the long run, influencing public policy.

The decline of the grassroots had roots of its own in the dramatic social changes that have taken place in America, and if we are nostalgic about the torchlight parades or the image of neighbors knocking on doors to bring the word about whom the party is running for office to those inside, let us hold those memories dear, but also recognize that far more accurate and in-depth information is beginning to get through to millions of voters in both parties. We might someday again have parades, but the odds are the marchers will be paid professionals, or at least organized by professionals.

The Way Back: What Works and What Doesn't

Both major national parties began embarking on changes that would take some years to bear fruit, but once ripened, would alter the entire structure of the party system. Although it is still true that neither party completely controls its own destiny, and both have minimal influence on the nomination of their presidential candidates, they are beginning to emerge as the single most effective participant in electoral politics outside the campaign organization.

One reason for the strength is to be found within the parties (albeit unevenly distributed at this point); another has to do with the constraints imposed on other players in the process. The campaign finance legislation, passed in the 1970s, seriously limited the role of other groups and, to a some extent, individual large contributors—the "fat cats" of whom we have heard so much. The federal law has been replicated in different ways in many of the states, and although it looked in the beginning as if the law was going to hurt the parties, especially the local grassroots parties, it seems to have been a major contributing factor to the new strength of the national party committees.

The third cause for the new party strength is the developing nature of campaign technology. The communications revolution, which has changed so much in our lives, has made it easier for a national organization to reach individuals throughout the nation, on the one hand, and on the other hand, it has forced greater reliance on technical ability and expertise. The permanent party organization is in a better position to secure the equipment, sustain the data, and know how to use it. Something of a political economy of scale.

In the following chapters we will explore the rebuilding process in some depth, but before we argue our case, we would like to consider some of the alternative routes—things that might have been—and why they did not occur.

LEADERSHIP

There is a certain ambivalence in suggesting that leadership can make the difference. Strong leadership has indeed changed the course of the parties from time-to-time (including this time), but the lack of leadership is not just the idiosyncratic failure of individuals charged with the task, it is built into the weak institution. Some circumstances are better suited to the emergence of leadership than others; some occasions call for different kinds of leaders.

There is no obvious path to political leadership. That we have found extraordinarily talented leaders in moments of need in the parties per se and in the political world at large is something of a mystery. For our purposes, we want to consider the impact of the office of the president on party development (and demise), and, secondarily, the capacity of the party organization to promote leaders of its own, both for the party and for nomination to elective office.

The President.   In theory, the president is the chief spokesman of his party as well as of the nation. Certainly he is the standard bearer. But his responsibility for the party as an organization does not appear to extend beyond his own re-election. Richard Nixon, as we noted, actively discouraged the GOP from supporting strong candidates against friendly members of Congress in the Democratic party. Nixon's efforts were neither unrealistic nor unique, given the need of a president to use every tool at his disposal to get his programs through congress, including trading with representatives of the opposite party.

Some of the crossing of party lines is due to the heterogeneity within the parties (although they are certainly more homogeneous today than they used to be): there are liberals (well, at least moderates) in both parties, and there are both Democratic and Republican conservatives. The heterogeneity is due partly to the parties' lack of control over their nominees, but is due mostly to the very real differences there are between regions in the country. Republicans Senator Lowell Weicker, (Connecticut) and Congressman Silvio Conte (Massachusetts) are far more liberal than members of Congress in either party from Mississippi or Alabama. If a national party expects to win control of Congress, it must accept the regional differences and support those candidates with the best chance of winning, even if they veer away from the party line on some issues. Even if that were not the case, the president has a responsibility to lead the whole country and bipartisan support will always be crucial to his success, especially if he is dealing with controversial issues or matters of foreign policy.

Another factor that is somewhat outside the party is the president's need to rely on interest groups and their networks of supporters and experts for policy development and implementation. The coalition he puts together to win election in the first place is largely based on issue groups and other identifiable interests in the population. Even if the interests lean heavily toward one party or the other, they have a separate organization and a separate set of players to whom the president must appeal and must respond when it comes to naming individuals to office in his administration.

Then there is the political process itself and the way a president comes to office. The primary places a premium on candidate organization, almost to the exclusion of party regulars. Presidential primaries do not always hurt a state party, but they certainly play on the differences within it as each faction lines up behind a different candidate, sometimes because this candidate represents their views, but just as often because the other candidate asked the other faction leader first. By the time a candidate wins the nomination, he has built an organization of his own in almost every state and then must face the task of building bridges to those within the party who supported his opponents. It is a Humpty Dumpty effort of putting the party back together again.

There are limits on the number of positions a presidential nominee can offer opposing state party leaders, and there can also be very real differences between the interests of a presidential candidate and the slate of candidates the state party is putting forth for the lesser offices. It has happened on more than one occasion that those most likely to vote for the presidential nominee would also be most likely to vote for the other party's senatorial or gubernatorial candidate. If that happens, where the money is spent to get out the vote makes a big difference.

We do not mean to imply that a president is necessarily an enemy to the party, although Jimmy Carter, for instance, did view the party as something of an albatross around his neck. But we do want to make the point that there are a number of valid, or at least understandable, reasons for a president to put his interests ahead of the party. It is not surprising that presidents not only rarely make strong party leaders, but they very often are the main impediment to strong national party leadership coming from within the party itself. The president and his party stand in a relationship of mutual dependence, but historically the marriage subordinates the long-term interests of the organization to the short-term needs of the president and his policies.

A story told by a member of the White House staff during the 1984 campaign highlights the nature of campaigning and some of the problems. Toward the end of the election—after the second debate—it was clear to both sides that Reagan was going to win re-election, and the decision was made in both camps to use the presidential candidate to bolster the prospects of congressional candidates. The day before the campaign ended, Reagan was in Wisconsin and some of his staff drove past an establishment named "Fritz's Bar." In the spirit that often overtakes campaign workers at the end of the day, they bethought themselves that it would be amusing if Reagan stopped in for a visit. This line of thought was carried to its natural conclusion that it would be amusing, and reasonable, if Reagan dropped in on neighboring Minnesota, Mondale's home state. Because being in the room when the decision is made is the most critical characteristic of any political decision, on the last day of the campaign, the schedule was changed and, instead of going to any of the other possible stops the schedulers back in Washington had been fighting over for weeks, the Reagan entourage made a brief stop in Minnesota to tell the people of that state that he cared for them, too. In retrospect, more than one party worker felt the stop cost them Nebraska where they lost a close election. No one will ever be able to prove it, but the choice, and the values that entered into the decision, are characteristic of the problem in the best of times.⁸ Watergate may be an example of the worst of times when the re-election of the president is linked in the minds of the presidential staff with the survival of the nation, which may have motivated the attempted break-in and cover-up.

Campaigns are generally dominated by the spending rule that more is more, but the campaign finance law has imposed some limits on what the national parties can do. Although the loopholes in the law are still impressive, and it turns out that the parties can do more than any other group, the combined national committees of each party (the national committee itself, plus the House and Senate campaign committees) now devote a good portion of their resources to nonpresidential elections in the quadrennial presidential cycle. In 1984, the national Republican party spent $3 million on state legislative races and supported to the maximum all of their House and Senate campaigns. Although the Democrats failed to raise the $6.9 million they were legally permitted to spend on behalf of the presidential election, they did raise considerable sums for voter registration and get-out-the-vote efforts, and the congressional campaign committees (especially the House committee) contributed to more Democratic candidates than ever before.

Because the law has limited the money the national party can spend on presidential elections (see the appendix for a fuller description on the federal campaign finance law), it has encouraged a kind of independence from the presidency, at least to the point of giving it a greater role in other elections. A role that is further enhanced by the fact that the law also limits what individuals can give to candidates and interest groups, and has therefore encouraged more party giving. Participating actively in other elections is not a surprising role for the national party, but it is a marked change from the historical function of existing principally for the purpose of electing a president.

Party Leaders. If the president will not lead, or at least has an ambivalent relationship with the party, what about the possibility of a leader emerging from among the ranks of party activists? Someone who will take hold of the organization and begin the rebuilding process? We have known great party leaders in the past: Mark Hanna, who built the Republican party into a majority party at the turn of the century; Boss Tweed, who ran Tammany Hall, perhaps not an entirely estimable character, but certainly an organizational leader.

One problem the political parties face in developing leadership is that they are not completely independent as organizations: they are subject to the behavior of outsiders and external events to a remarkable degree. The GOP had almost nothing to do with the Nixon re-election campaign, for instance, but the party as an organization suffered tremendously with the advent of Watergate. Party chairpersons tend to be close personal friends of the president or the leading presidential candidate. The direction of their loyalty, consequently, may not be entirely clear. And even if their objectives are beyond question, the ability to control the organization requires extraordinary skill because it is so diffuse and so many strands are connected elsewhere. It is a weak system for promoting leaders and it has resulted in a weak organization.

Party chairpersons, in years when the party does not hold the White House, have a different role to play from party chairpersons whose tenure in office coincides with control of the administration. In the off years, the party chairperson has a greater opportunity to exert leadership, but he or she must also be constantly mindful of balancing the interests of the leading presidential contenders. The role of the party chairperson lends itself, in other words, to being more like walking a tightrope than charging up San Juan Hill.

Still, sometimes strong leadership does emerge. Bill Brock, for instance, was very much responsible for turning the Republican National Committee (RNC) around in the post-Watergate years, building on the effective groundwork laid by his predecessors Ray Bliss (1965–1969) and Mary Louise Smith (1974–1976), particularly. Although there does not appear to have been much thought given to this topic by scholars so far, it would seem that the most important reason Brock was successful—beyond his personal strengths as an organization leader—was the fact that just before he acceded to the post, when the party held the administration, the incumbent was not strong enough to dominate the party. President Ford had never run for national office before, and he was challenged by a strong contender in Ronald Reagan. Neither presidential contender was powerful enough to control the party apparatus, and it gave Mary Louise Smith breathing space which Brock used to build upon while the Democrats were in office.

Similar circumstances may come to pass for both parties in the years between 1984 and 1988, when the field will be wide open in both parties among those seeking the presidential nomination. It is an opportunity the Democrats, most of all, could use to advantage in catching up to Republican party strength.

Another factor which may have aided Brock was that the party was so demoralized that there was a climate for change. The RNC created a series of issue task forces, which brought together the spectrum of Republican opinion but focused on consensus. Similar efforts by Democrats, such as the off-year issue conventions, have been carried out in the midst of public attention and are not especially conducive to compromise (the fact that the delegates were elected to the convention because of their stands on issues probably also made consensus harder to come by).

The problem of leadership is not always viewed as a problem. Most of the reforms directed at the parties over the years have sought to limit strong leadership, or put another way, were designed to get rid of the bosses. Some would argue that given our distrust of power, a weak party organization is the best kind to have. Certainly the reforms were aimed at controlling the influence of party leaders on the selection of party nominees, appointments to office, and just about every other perk of power the parties used to enjoy. As it happens, however, most political scientists and most observers and participants in politics do not believe a weak system is best. David Broder's primary thesis was that the party—and only the party—would be able to move the society beyond the troubles it has faced for the past thirty years.

The issue of party weakness and the expectations surrounding it, from those who do not trust power to those who want to see more, is itself an important factor in the question of party leadership. Because the parties are held in low esteem they are not likely to attract the best potential leaders. This is hardly a startling conclusion, but it is one that must be stated. At the local level, where parties are their weakest, the "best" people in town participate in civic associations. The state level is a bit higher up on the scale, and the national level considerably higher, but we doubt there are many small boys and girls today in America who think they want to grow up to chair the national party.

If the parties were perceived to have power, there might be something worth fighting for. Although we think the parties have more power now than they have ever had before, as a nation we are still influenced by the belief that they are weak. If that attitude should change, the pool of potential leaders would enlarge and improve. The fact that the 1985 selection of a Democratic chairman was a hard-fought campaign waged by more than a half-dozen contenders suggests the prize was valued highly by at least some.

THE GRASSROOTS

Our images of the political parties are conflicting. We see cigar-smoke and backrooms, and we see torchlight parades and Fourth of July orators. Sometimes we can recall these scenes from childhood, sometimes we see them through a haze and they seem cloaked in a turn-of-the-century costume. We have held the image in our hearts (and in the movies), but they have been in decline ever since the Progressive Era.

Most observers use the decline of grassroots politics as a measure of the decline of the parties—and they may be right to do so. It is just that they tend to blame the backroom politicians and not the reformers for the death. The reformers went after the politicians for a number of good and honorable reasons, and we could, therefore, place the blame indirectly on the "pols," but the problem in doing so is that it obscures the nature of the grassroots organizations: what maintained them, and why they no longer function.

Concern about the health of the local parties goes to the notion of democracy. Their decline is seen as a breakdown in continuity, a lessening of the legitimacy of all government, and a threat to the stability of the society. Nelson Polsby, a very astute political scientist at the University of California who recognized the centralized nature of the new party structure fairly early on, has also become a major voice of concern about the consequences.

According to Polsby, the parties have become labels for "masses of individual voters who pick among various candidates in primary elections as they would among any alternatives marketed by the mass media."[9] Because the parties gather their resources now through direct mail and media campaigns, "they have displaced in importance the mobilizing of well-heeled backers and the seeking of alliances with territorially identifiable interest groups and state party organizations." Candidate-based organizations have replaced the dependence on "party regulars and state and local party leaders."[10] Although we share his concern about candidate-based organizations, we believe they are on the way out, as national and state party organizations become stronger, and (we must admit we are writing a few years after he drew his observations) we do not share his view of the consequences of the decline of local parties.

What concerns Polsby is the changing nature of interest group activity: the declining role of traditional groups which are organized around economic issues or the "communal ties" of their membership; the rise of groups which appear to possess a "disinterested rectitude" (such as Common Cause), and those representing the "historically disadvantaged such as black, Hispanic-American and militant women's groups."[11] While a number of these groups seem to represent the grassroots, it is a misrepresentation to Polsby; they are the creation of the mass media and that is where their power lies.

There are negative consequences of this change. Because the media is the base of power, negotiations among groups or with the government must be carried out publicly. Responsible leaders are forced to announce their positions and are, therefore, hampered, if not completely prevented, from reaching a compromise, or even coming to a serious understanding of the other side. "Participants are tempted into confrontation politics and moralism in order to look good."

> In a large-scale society based upon appeals from leaders to followers for their votes, it is evidently inescapable that some sort of division of labor will take place in which people specialize in working for mediating institutions that are separate from leaders and followers and undertake to link them. What sorts of institutions these are, what sorts of values infuse their management, what sorts of messages they spread and retard are bound to have political consequences and will influence the relations between leaders and their publics.[12]

The intermediary agents who have been replaced by the media interpret the interest of ordinary people to their leaders and tutor the people in the alternatives available to them. They educate the citizenry to its rights and responsibilities, and assure legitimacy for the regime. Such traditional agents include the family (both nuclear and extended), school, primary work and social groups, voluntary associations that promote shared interests, and, of course, political representatives. What makes these groups intermediaries is that the communication flows both ways. What makes television dangerous, or at least unusually powerful, is that the communication is directed only one way, hence increasing the impact of its values.

While Polsby acknowledges that the political parties, along with most of the other traditional intermediary structures, are engaged in the same business of trying to influence the media on the one hand, and using the technology to sustain themselves on the other, he believes they are losing the loyalty of voters. "To say that political parties are in trouble is mostly to say little more than that state and local party elites have lost influence over some of the processes most important in their collective life, such as the making of political—especially presidential—nominations." It is not so much the rise in the number of interest groups that Polsby fears, as it is the decline of the capacity of party leaders to "resist, channel, accommodate, or limit the demands of these groups for extraordinary influence over the presidential nomination process."[13]

We agree that the state and local parties have lost the capacity to influence the presidential selection (which we ascribe principally to the number of primaries and caucuses), but we think other things have happened to the parties that are important, such as influencing every other nomination, and we think that the loss of influence of the structures he is describing, particularly the local party, is not a loss we can do very much about. It is a self-contained loss that has not seriously damaged the ability of the political parties to perform the functions about which he is concerned. We will describe the role and the decline of local parties in a later chapter in much more detail, but would like for the moment to accept his premise that the local parties are in bad straits and consider some alternative reactions to the news.

When the local parties were more powerful, they did have a good deal of influence in national politics. Local party bosses could wheel and deal among themselves and select a nominee for the presidency, often a strong candidate who could and would represent the interests of the mainstream of the party. Their interest was in winning because with victory came the spoils, enabling them to take care of their followers and maintain their organizations. It was just that power that led to most of the party reforms at the close of the last and the beginning of this century. Or, perhaps, more accurately, it was the power such bosses held over their local communities—a power not as nobly exercised as it might have been at the presidential level where the rewards were more distant and vague—that fostered the momentum toward curtailing it.

We would not like to suggest that all local party leaders were less than idealistically-oriented, but neither would we like to accept the notion that all strong local parties consistently served the public good. Beyond the presidential nominating convention, there was little for the national parties to do. They tended to lie there like wet blankets at the top of the party organization pyramid. Perhaps they could have done more—mediating at the federal level for instance —but they did not. In fact, the structure of the party system was weak throughout, characterized more by autonomy than accountability.

Today the influence runs the other way around: the national party is a full-time, professional organization, which provides sustenance to the state and local parties. The Republican party, particularly, has become active in the selection and support of candidates for Congress and, occasionally, for state and local office as well. We think there are signs that the national parties can regain influence over the presidential selection process and would point to the fact that Walter Mondale—whatever weaknesses he may have had as a candidate for the Democratic party in 1984—came out of the center of the party. He was not an outsider, he did not represent a fringe element in the party. If the "old system" were in operation, Mondale would have been the most likely nominee.

The problem of fewer mediating institutions in the political process with which Polsby is concerned does not really address the question of what happens when the national party comes into the process. It is our view that when the Republican National Committee, or either of its House or Senate Campaign Committees, enters a race, its motivation is to promote a winner: someone whose appeal extends beyond those who represent controversial minority views.

Most successful organizations in this country (at least until recently) seem to be built on a pyramid-shaped structure, bureaucratically rationalizing the distribution of power, effectively and efficiently focusing their resources and maximizing whatever it is they are in the business of maximizing (profits, membership growth, out-put, sales, and so on). The parties have been somewhat anachronistic (not to say archaic) in their structure, and it is not surprising, therefore, that the absence of the strengths of the bureaucratic model have been felt, leaving the parties subject to external pressures far more than to internal focus.

It is more probable that there is a stronger relationship between the various levels of the party today than there used to be, and even though the direction of influence is from the top down, it is not an isolated exercise of power. There is communication and there is involvement by the party as an organization. Through direct mail solicitations there is also the participation of millions of citizens who consider themselves party members because they contribute to it. It is not local, but it is real.

For good or ill, the old system no longer survives. Local party organizations cannot find strong leaders, they cannot mount armies of workers who will man the posts of precinct captains and function as ward healers. The population from which they drew their leaders and their workers no longer exists. The population they served no longer needs them, at least not the way they did before. On the other hand, some of the functions of the old system have been transferred from the local to the national level. The national party, as intermediary between voters and public officials may not be as homey as local party workers, but it can certainly communicate, educate, and instill loyalty in the political system. If there is to be a return to local volunteers, they will be organized by the professionals who reach out to them with appeals they know will work. In 1984, the Republican party estimated that it turned out 600,000 volunteers in support of the Reagan/Bush campaign. The fact that it cost between $9 and $10 million to do it suggests that it takes more than popular support of the president to bring volunteers out, and most of the activities were supplemented with paid workers.

There is a good possibility that the national party can be a far more effective manager of party affairs (including the provision of resources to build and sustain strong state party organizations) than the old system was. Not all states and localities had strong, competitive parties; the relationship between localities and states was not always compatible.

If accountability is one of the characteristics of a system based on intermediary structures, one must question how accountable the old system was and consider the possibility that there may just be more accountability under the new system because the money and the voting support comes from the bottom. It is something of which the professionals at the top are quite mindful. Elections, after all, occur on a regular basis.

The question of how the national party will use its influence remains somewhat open. Will it be more interested in maintaining ideological purity or will it be more interested in winning elections? We believe there is evidence to suggest that the professional party apparatus will lean toward winning office.

THE VOTERS

Polsby feels that the loss of intermediary structures is largely responsible for the decline in voter identification with the parties. Although he recognizes that the decline in party loyalty might be due to other causes,[14] he still believes it has an impact because the new system discourages coalition building and favors factionalism in the presidential selection, or because of the way the presidential contest is conducted: through the media, with little face-to-face interaction (with the possible exceptions of Iowa and New Hampshire where the voters are probably inundated with candidate interaction). Recognizing that some "mechanisms may be reasonably efficient as devices for informing candidates, . . . they are bound to be less comprehensively engaging to at least some ordinary voters than more personalized organizational structures."[15] What all of this leads to, according to Polsby, is a loss of political legitimacy, which is reflected in the growing disaffection with our presidents and the general sense of "ungovernability," or the inability of government leaders to lead.

There is a correlation between partisan identification and belief in the system (see chapter 6).[16] The curious phenomenon about the correlation is that it is not clear which way the causality goes: it may be that partisan loyalty encourages confidence; it may be that confidence permits partisan loyalty. But for those who are not strong partisans, it is very clear there has been a marked decrease in confidence in all institutions in the past several decades.

We would agree that the primary system favors factionalism, and that disaffection with the candidates who make it through the primaries to nomination is an important factor in the unwillingness of voters to support the parties, or at least their party's nominee. We do not accept, however, the notion that because the primary is carried out through the media instead of face-to-face it affects the legitimacy. First of all, it is not the candidate with whom the voter would meet (in the old days, the candidate tended to stay home), so what we are talking about is the party canvasser, who has been replaced by paid and unpaid television coverage, by direct mail campaigns, telephones, and whatever volunteers the campaign can muster and back up with professional help.

There is certainly something personal about having someone come to your door to talk to you about the party's candidates. It undoubtedly provides a greater sense of being "part of the process." But voters still draw conclusions about candidates, they still talk to their friends and family (intermediary structures that have not entirely disappeared), and they may be getting far more accurate information about the candidate and the party's position on issues.

As the technology improves, messages can be targeted to very specific groups through the use of cable television, which reaches a more definable audience and has the capacity to permit some measure of two-way communication. The targeting of messages by zip code, and any other number of devices used in marketing, knows almost no bounds. We believe the increase in information counteracts the loss of a neighbor's visit, and we also believe that the neighbor will not be coming back.

There is one exception: local elections. Local candidates for office still go door-to-door themselves and can still call upon neighbors to walk with them or for them. The problem for the parties is that very few of these elections are partisan. If we want to increase partisan involvement, we would have to change the structure of these elections.

The subject of partisan identification is an entire subfield in political science, some of which we will address in the chapter on voters. It is our contention that while partisan identification has declined, partisan behavior has remained relatively stable: We still include party affiliation of the candidates in our calculation of how to cast our vote. We also believe that strong partisanship is correlated to strong parties. The weak parties of the recent past had little with which to attract new generations of voters. The parties we see today, and the parties we expect to see in the future, will be far more effective in seeking adherents, educating them to the principles for which they stand, and assuring a greater measure of stability and legitimacy in the system.

Strong parties, by our definition, would have control over the nomination of their candidates for office and would exist for the purpose of contesting election and influencing public policy. In order for them to attain these objectives, they need control over resources, an effective organizational structure, and a special role to play in the democracy. Until recently, they have endured almost entirely because of their role in the legal structuring of elections in the states where gaining access to the ballot has required some form of party endorsement, and in the structure they provide for the work of almost every legislature in the country.

The outline of the new party system is already in place. It differs from the old in the degree of internal control it exercises over its candidates and over the face it presents to voters. It is not immune to the pressures of external interests, but it seeks more actively to incorporate the interests into its processes, leaving less and less room for third parties to develop, which might otherwise use the energy of the excluded groups to challenge the hegemony of the two major parties. Incorporating the interests makes the parties seem to be the captive of extremists (Republicans by the Moral Majority, for instance; Democrats by the activists in civil rights for minorities, women, and homosexuals). In the end, it is the party which chews up and digests the interests.

The notion that the parties today are different is an idea that has been slow in gaining recognition among the scholars and journalists whose business it is to report upon such things. We seem to find it easier to grasp in the specifics but lose sight of when it comes to generalities. There will be a newspaper story that candidate X could not get party backing and withdrew from the primary in the same article that discourses upon the weak party system in America. There have been untold numbers of articles on the millions of dollars pouring into the national Republican party committees, or the thousands of participants in Democratic precinct meetings to choose delegates to the national presidential nominating conventions, but no one will declare the parties to be alive and well.

Those who work in politics on a day-to-day basis are more at home with the idea that there has been a change, but the awareness has been slow to seep out to the public at large. Perhaps it is one of the Basic Truths of Life that if change comes slowly, recognition of change is even slower.

Part of the problem may be due to the complexity of the political world, which leaves almost everything in a state of ambiguity. Or, perhaps, we just do not like to think very much about the parties. We have always been moderately suspicious of politics and have rarely held politicians and the political parties in great esteem. Democracy is an ideal that we fail to attain so, characteristically, we seem to prefer alienation.

It is our belief that whether or not we think the parties ought to be strong, we should be aware of what has happened in the past decade to change the political parties and, as a result, the entire political system. It is our hope that this book will help dispel some of the myths about our politics.

In the following chapters we will tell the story of how the parties got into the terrible straits David Broder described in the early 1970s: the ambivalence about power that has accompanied us throughout our history; the ravages of reform, some intended, some not. We will note the passage of generations and the changes in ourselves, as well as our institutions, that affect our politics. We will describe the new system: power flowing from the national level down; strong, professional organizations capable of harnessing power and focusing policy. We will consider what that power is and what makes it effective. In the last part, we will consider the world of organized interests and unorganized voters. We will place the party system in context and consider the future.

2

Decline and Fall

.

TINKERING with the process seems to be an inherent characteristic of American democracy. Most of the pressure for change comes from the ever-changing nature of the population: immigration, industrialization, urbanization, suburbanization, and so on. Some of the pressure is due to a distrust of power imbedded deeply within us. Concepts of freedom and individuality, which have been so much a part of the American dream, require the most restrained use of power. The fear of power has characterized political life since the Revolution. Just about all of our reforms were directed at the devolution of power, taking it from those at the center and distributing it as widely as possible. It took us a century and a half, but we finally succeeded in constraining the organized mobilization for power: the parties. We reformed them to the point where the structure of organization was a shadow, and after that, we began to worry about the fragmentation of interests, the alienation of the citizenry, and the fragility of our institutions.

It has become axiomatic in politics to expect "unintended consequences" from reform. It is not just that we fail to understand the role of the various participants, it is that the system itself is so complex, so ambiguous, new needs are inevitably identified and new opportunities emerge. A curtailment of the power of business affects labor, and typically, it is labor which starts the process only to find it backfires later on. If reform is motivated out of fear of the power of others, curtailing that power seems only to unleash it elsewhere. When we weakened the parties, we left more power unchecked in the interests.

A DEFINITION OF PARTY DECLINE

Most accounts of the death of the parties refer to the decline of partisan identification in the population. That is an important factor, but it is probably more an effect than a cause, and if we want to understand why the parties declined, we must consider the relationship between the reforms and the decline. Party decline must also be measured against party strength. If one can accept the broader definition of parties (see chapter 1) then they can be said to exist for the purpose of influencing government by controlling nominations and resources, and contesting elections. Therefore, we can say that the parties have declined if they have experienced:

- *A loss in their control over nominations*—Without the capacity to put forth candidates upon whom the voters can rely to represent party principles, the election of any given candidate to any given office becomes an idiosyncratic experience. Without dependence on the party for nomination, no office holder need respond to party demands for the support of party programs.
- *A loss in their control of resources*—Providing resources for campaigns are one way the party influences candidates, both in the nature of the resources (such as research and issue material) and in the dependence on the party the expenditure of money evokes in candidates toward the party. Another use resources have been put to in the past has been as an incentive for party participation: the material gain party workers could expect to follow an election victory, from jobs, to contracts, to help in dealing with government bureaucracies. If candidates find their money elsewhere, if the party is useless in helping the faithful, its value to them declines.
- *A reduced ability to contest elections*—If elections are not organized as a contest between the parties, their function obviously disappears, as it has quite notably in most cities and towns across the nation where nonpartisan elections are the order of the day.

- *A reduced ability to influence government*—If the parties are thought to have no program for action, no sense of how the group out of power would alter things once in power, they provide little incentive for anyone to join them, either as a candidate or as a voting supporter. We need to believe in the ability of the party to govern in order to elect it.
- *A rise in the unpredictability of voting behavior*—If allegiance to the parties declines among the voters because the parties have little to hold them, and they have lost the habit of thinking of political events in terms of the parties, there will be an increase of issue groups and a flux of candidates for office running on their personal characteristics rather than their commitments to a philosophy (however broadly defined) of government. Elections will become discreet experiences, and alienation from the political system may increase.

All of these functions, including the objective of standing for a set of principles, cannot be maintained unless there is some central core that makes decisions, chooses candidates, and allocates the resources. The strength of the party is, therefore, dependent on the strength of the organization. It must be able to select leaders and determine its rules of behavior. The only areas where the parties have remained consistently strong have been in the state legislatures and in Congress, where the organization does just that: determines its leadership and its processes. The area where the parties at large have become the weakest is in their ability to sustain effective organizations that function on a permanent basis. Following all this has been the declining loyalty to the party by the voters.

PARTY DECLINE: THE WAY IT HAPPENED

In the course of this century, the parties have lost considerable control over their nominations with the spread of the primary. Nowhere is that more obvious than at the presidential level where the proliferation of primaries in the past two decades has made the nominating conventions an exercise in showmanship for the victor rather than a trading of power by party leaders to select the best candidate. For the Democrats, the nomination of Jimmy Carter was probably the nadir of party influence because the former Georgia governor ran for office as a nonparty candidate. Coming from the South where the parties have behaved more like factions, he had little experience of effective parties and no reason to change his mind given the nominating process which required him to create his own organization, roaming from caucus to primary around the country.

At the congressional level, the adherence to the party ticket among voters has been falling steadily throughout the century. In 1900, 3.4 percent of the electorate split their vote; the figure rose to 32.8 percent in 1980 (after a high of 44.1 percent in 1972).[1]

As parties have come to play less of a role in candidate selection and become less a predictor of voting behavior, so, too, have they grown less attractive to donors, who would prefer to give directly to the candidates. Although the situation is markedly different today, up until the mid-1970s, the parties were either in debt or operating near the poverty line. Under those conditions, they were unable to offer very much to their candidates, to their workers, or to the public at large. It is particularly true at the local level where problems for the parties have been compounded with the emergence of nonpartisan elections for the vast majority of cities and towns.

There is no question that the parties have declined. Our task is to understand why they have declined: which historical events, reforms, and changes in the social structure brought that decline about.

The Reform Efforts

There were three important periods of reform: the revolt against the caucus system for selecting the presidential nominee in the early part of the nineteenth century; the Progressive Era (by far the most critical in determining the strength of the parties in our century); and the latest period in the 1970s, which saw the passage of campaign finance regulation. We will address the impact of the law (which we believe to have been beneficial) in the appendix and devote this chapter to the earlier efforts to change the parties and to the external factors, which were not designed to weaken the parties, but had that effect nonetheless.

THE REVOLT AGAINST KING CAUCUS

No president was as hostile to the concept of parties as George Washington. To the first chief executive, the development of political parties was a failure of the unification achieved with the new constitution and government. He must have felt the failure even more keenly because the first party system developed around the personalities of Alexander Hamilton and Thomas Jefferson, members of his cabinet. The competition among the Federalists, led by Hamilton (but with Washington as titular head), and the Republican/Democrats (which became the Democratic party we know today) led by Jefferson, ended with the domination of the latter group by the early years of the nineteenth century.

Although it is clear in hindsight that the creation of the parties enabled the majority to demonstrate its will in an orderly fashion and settle differences peaceably, including the transition of power, it was a time of great uncertainty. We had just succeeded in revolution and were building a new world without benefit of tradition and tested relationships.

A constant source of tension in the early years of the United States was the need for a national government—and all that entailed in speaking with one voice, establishing relationships with foreign nations, assuring interstate commerce, and so on on the one hand, and the autonomy and self-direction by the large separated regions that made up the new nation on the other hand. The first government, the Confederation, failed. According to one historian, "Americans misjudged the extent to which independence required the centralization of authority." The Constitution rectified the situation to some extent, but "it provided no mechanism for focusing national attention on the pressing issues of the day or for collecting popular sentiment. The first political parties, offsprings of a national center of decision-making performed that task."[2] Under the Confederation, decisions were made at the state level, and it was there that political divisions occurred and were resolved. But centralization, particularly in a large country with poor communication, created a need, which the parties met, for structured institutions capable of managing conflict.[3]

According to historian Paul Goodman, the new party system

played a "critical role in providing a means for various groups to influence decision making through alliances with others which gave them effective political striking power, and in promoting trust and willingness to compromise among disparate forces separated by parochial perspectives and preferences."⁴ The parties made it possible to replace the deferential style of politics carried on in the courthouses and state capitols of the colonies and Confederation where face-to-face meetings occurred among persons who knew each other's place in the society.

The more centralized the decision making became, the greater became the need for formal channels of expression and compromise, because the men who made the decisions, and those who were affected, no longer knew each other. The parties were successful in bridging the problem of communications and understanding, but they never completely allayed the fear of power and the uncertainty many Americans felt about its exercise.

Throughout the 1790s, many citizens of the United States believed the future of the nation was threatened. This insecurity was the major cause of "widespread, deep, and fierce partisan sentiments." Once the continued existence of the nation and the transition of power were secured, with the election in 1800 of the first non-Federalist, Thomas Jefferson, partisanship declined dramatically and the Federalists effectively passed away from the national scene. It may be one of the ironies of history that it was the Federalists who believed in elite decision making and the Republicans who were hostile to the notion of national authority.

Whatever the philosophical differences between the first two parties, it is clear that a major reason for the decline in partisanship was the belief held by both sides that they were not professional politicians. Once the nation felt itself secure and the cause of partisanship passed, the need to maintain the structures passed with it. Both sides thought of themselves as statesmen rather than politicians, and so the party leaders returned home, following the lead of Washington, who declined the crown he was offered by the grateful nation and retired to Mount Vernon at the end of the Revolution. They maintained an extensive correspondence with their compatriots, but no one really believed in the need to sustain the organization through which they had affected power.

The expectation that statesmen are above partisan feeling has been characteristic of American political life throughout our history. The heterogeneity of the nation has always made homogeneity a goal: we want to think of ourselves as united, as having a common view and a common purpose. The very idea of parties is an anathema to those who believe the nation is best served by dedication to the highest, and therefore most united, objective. This attitude permeates our sense of politics. We believe ourselves to be at our best when there is no disagreement; we are succumbing to baser, more private motives when there is dispute. It is an element in the antiparty feeling we have carried with us as a society from the beginning, although it may be rooted in deeper psychological causes.

The death of the Federalist party as a contender for the presidency (which some may have construed as a civic virtue because it meant less division in the nation) in practical terms meant that whoever was nominated by the Republicans became president. Belief in our unity was balanced by concern for the unrestrained exercise of power. It was the making of the first wave of reform.

Beginning in 1800, when Alexander Hamilton called the first caucus of his party's representatives in Congress to promote Thomas Pinckney over John Adams (because he was afraid that Washington's vice-president was too much of a pacifist and would not be able to defeat Jefferson), both parties used the caucus as a vehicle for decision making. The caucus was an informal gathering of party leaders (typically members of Congress, but including others), which met to plan strategy and choose candidates. Our legislatures still make a variety of decisions, including leadership decisions, in party caucuses, with the selection of the majority party usually being tantamount to election as that body's speaker. It is an informal way of finding consensus, and it is a powerful mechanism because its decisions come to represent the formal organization. The choice of the caucus became the party's nominee and his name was put forward in the formal electoral process.

The caucus system became most vulnerable at the close of James Monroe's second term in 1824. Monroe was the last president in the Virginia dynasty (which included Washington, Jefferson, and James Madison). He succeeded to his position in what is called

"The Era of Good Feeling," when the Federalists were at their weakest and there was still unity in the Republican party. There was, however, no clear successor and the nomination for president was hotly contested by five candidates: John Quincy Adams, John C. Calhoun, Henry Clay, William G. Crawford, and Andrew Jackson. Crawford, a Georgian, stood to gain most by the congressional caucus, and his state legislature expressed both their support for him and their belief that the caucus was the only legitimate method of nomination.

Because caucus nomination was tantamount to election, and because there were a number of candidates, the system was challenged by the other candidates and their supporters, who denounced "King Caucus" and urged the members of Congress not to attend it. When the caucus met, only 66 of the 216 Republican congressmen participated, and they nominated Crawford for president and Albert Gallatin for vice-president as expected. Crawford won forty-one votes in the electoral college, carrying only Georgia and Virginia. Jackson, who represented the most democratic instincts, won with ninety-nine votes, followed by Adams with eighty-four (all from New England), and Clay coming in at the bottom with thirty-seven votes.[5]

The electoral system at the time gave the electoral college a greater role than it appears to have today in selecting the president. Suffrage was limited to white, propertied males, and the delegates to the electoral college were chosen in a variety of methods, from election by district, statewide election of the individual electors, or selection by state legislatures. It was expected that the states would pick their most distinguished citizens to serve as electors, who would play a deliberative role in selecting the president.

The emergence of the parties and their role in choosing a candidate was not anticipated by the authors of the Constitution. The caucus, and later the convention, effectively replaced the electoral college as the forum for deliberation. In time, the parties chose the electors, with a winner-take-all system by which all of the state's electors were selected by the party winning a plurality within the state. Although not required to do so by law, the electors are now expected to follow the party lead and formalize the popular vote.

While there is no question that the immediate cause of the

reform was the pressure of candidates not likely to benefit from the existing system, one of the reasons for its success must be that it was couched in terms likely to appeal to a broader spectrum of Americans, who were skeptical about parties, and perhaps a little concerned about the distance between themselves and their representatives. Every reform appeal made since has been based on the need to control the power of backroom politicians and broaden participation by the electorate.

THE PROGRESSIVE ERA

The Progressive Era (generally understood to include the period between 1900 and the First World War) was a time of extraordinary change and adjustment in American history. If one could argue that it was a failure of the political system that led to the Civil War, it was certainly true that during the forty years following the war, politics remained in the background, and American life was dominated by a great burst of private energy and almost-unprecedented entrepreneurship. It was the era of the Robber Barons, who linked the country with railroads and created an industrial society. One historian characterized it as a time of "intense partisanship and massive political indifference":

> With the order of things so uncertain, party identification gave men a common label, a comfortable rhetoric, to share with their group; it might also provide some sort of national attachment at a time when any rewarding ties between the community and the world beyond were rare indeed. Moreover, politics served as a grand recreational device, a reason for picnics and rallies, social busy work and oratorical festivities, without the restraining hand of the pastor or the employer.[6]

At the same time, immigration continued and increased dramatically with the unrest in Eastern Europe. The essentially rural country that went to war with itself in the 1860s became an urban nation, populated by strangers with differing cultures, expectations, and needs.

Joseph Nye, a Harvard political scientist, in a fascinating article on corruption in developing nations, suggested that corruption is a necessary element in the development of nations because in the early stages of development, societies lack the infrastructures necessary to make things work. Entrepreneurs who bend the rules can bring together the resources they need to create development. The system becomes dysfunctional only when a middle class and/or a student population emerges, because those groups, more than anyone else, believe in morality and law.[7]

The Progressive Era was the triumph of the middle class over the corruption of the Gilded Age. By the turn of the century, Americans were pausing to take stock of what had happened to them. Although energy and an unbounded belief in possibilities still characterized the nation as a whole, the realization was beginning to dawn for many that white-collar lives lived in large, anonymous corporations were not going to lead to great riches or much prestige. The new urban middle class entered the political fray to impose morality and order on a system gone seriously awry.

One of the first objects of Progressive reform was the political party that had reached a kind of zenith in urban machines (such as Tammany Hall in New York and the Prendergast organization in Kansas City) and new national strength under the leadership of Republican Mark Hanna.

The Republican party dominated the nation and undercut the growing progressive/populist movement among small white southern and midwestern farmers. Among Hanna's innovations was the imposition of a tithe on business to the Republican party. The story goes that major corporations were expected to send in their donations and if Mr. Hanna thought the money insufficient, he asked for more. If he thought the donation excessive, he returned it.

The Progressives, who were characteristically hostile to large impersonal organizations such as the corporations that had come to control so much of American economic life, were hostile to the corruption of local machines as well as the new relationship between those corporations and the national Republican party. The situation was undoubtedly exacerbated by the attempt of some corporations to turn members of Congress from representatives of their local parties and constituencies into representatives of national business interests (it is not an unknown charge in these days of Political Action Committee (PAC) fund raising either). At the national level, the reforms led to the Tillman Act of 1907, which prohibited corporate contributions. The legislation followed the

1904 election of Theodore Roosevelt, which revealed Hanna's assessments policy.

Although there were several bills passed in the next few years in
Congress, the most important focus of the Progressive reforms of
the parties was directed at the local level (aside from the fund
raising, the activities of the national party were rather negligible):
the ballot, the primary as a method of selecting candidates, and
nonpartisan elections. All three succeeded and had a tremendous
impact on the decline of the political parties for the next fifty years.

The Australian Ballot.   Prior to the Progressive Era, voters
would come to the poll and ask for a ballot by party. Clearly, ticket
splitting was impossible under such a system and the entire procedure left many voters subject to intimidation by partisan supporters. The new ballot, named for its place of origin, was printed by
public authority, as opposed to the party, and contained the names
of the candidates of all parties. The earliest advocates of the ballot
included labor and other minority groups who felt their political
strength undercut by the existing system. It was introduced in
Louisville, Kentucky in 1880, and was widely in use by 1900,
although it was not universally applied until 1950, when South
Carolina became the last state to adopt it.[8]

According to American Enterprise Institute scholar Austin
Ranney, it was the adoption of the Australian ballot that led to the
conversion of state and local parties from private associations to
public institutions.[9] It was the beginning of a long process of state
regulation: "Since a party label appears next to each candidate's
name on the ballot, it was said, it is necessary to be sure who is
legally entitled to it. Since the parties are benefited by having the
ballots say which candidate belongs to the parties, they must accept
the regulations necessary to ensure proper conduct of their
affairs."[10] He goes on to cite Robert LaFollette's gubernatorial
message to the Wisconsin legislature in 1903 as an expression of
the prevailing attitude among the leading Progressives:

> Every established practice and custom which tends to impair in any
> degree the citizens' right of suffrage subverts the principles of repre-
> sentative government and undermines the foundations of democracy.

... There are important proceedings, vitally essential to the right of suffrage, which are foundational, not only to manhood suffrage, but to the whole structure of government itself. What transpires back of the moment when the voter receives his official ballot must be as strongly fortified and as sacredly guarded as that which follows the consummation of this right after he receives the official ballot. ... If by bad practice and bad laws all the proceedings which control in the making of the ballot to be voted are taken out of the hands of the voter, his right of suffrage is not only impaired, but he has been deprived of it.[11]

Once the concept of regulating the parties began to take effect, many of the states went on to decide their organizational structure, qualification for membership, and rules for obtaining party office. Although the issue of self-determination is again up for debate—with the momentum going toward the parties—the swing in the Progressive Era was clearly toward public control.

The Direct Primary. Wisconsin, which was one of the most progressive states of the era, was also the site of the second major reform of the parties. The primary took the selection of a party's candidates out of the hands of its leaders and gave it to party members who made their selection in state-administered elections. According to one of the most prominent political scientists of the twentieth century, V. O. Key, Jr., the direct primary was particularly suited to the ideology of the period: "To [the Progressives] ... the direct primary constituted a means by which an enlightened people might cut through the mesh of organized and privileged power and grasp control of government. They had a faith that the people, once equipped with the proper weapons, would throw from office the rascals in possession of the city halls and state houses."[12] The primary was first employed on a statewide basis in Wisconsin in 1903, and by 1917, it was in use by all but a handful of states.[13]

Key attributes the spread of the primary to more than just the righteous indignation of the citizenry. He suggests that the weakness of state party structures was also an important factor. When Mark Hanna rebuilt the Republican party in the closing decade of the nineteenth century, the new alignment led to a fairly consistent pattern of single party domination in the states, which in turn led to a decline in the organizational strength of state parties as fac-

tions arose within the states. Competition among the factions prevented organizational stability, and opposing parties were often
controlled by the same interests that "owned the principal party."[14]

The primary was the most important reform affecting control of
nominations by parties, particularly in those states which adopted
the "open" primary, in which voters registered as independents, or
members of opposing parties, can participate in a party's selection
of its candidates even though the election is still organized by
party. It has been known, for example, for a party to encourage its
members to vote in the opposing party's primary for the purpose
of selecting the candidate most likely to be beaten in the general
election.

While the machines remained strong, party leaders were still
able to turn out their supporters to elect preferred candidates, but
as a reform it reflected the consistent themes of decentralizing the
process as well as the fears and prejudices against the party bosses.

The effect of the primary, while destructive, was not entirely
devastating. Not all offices are subject to primaries as a selection
process. In many instances, especially if there is an incumbent
running for re-election, there is only one candidate (there is an
argument to be made that even incumbents should be subject to
party review and discipline as occasionally happens in Minnesota).
In recent years, presidential primaries have been helpful in rebuilding parties in states dominated by the other party. Republican
parties in the South, for instance, draw energy and attention to
themselves on such occasions. Voter turnout is typically lower in
primaries than in general elections, and thus favors candidates who
can draw on some organization (including the party).

On the other hand, the proliferation of primaries in the presidential selection process has made many aware of the unfortunate
consequences of relying on a particular segment of the population:
the winner in a primary contest is not necessarily representative of
the interests of the mainstream of the party and may be in the
weakest of all positions to represent the party in the general election.

Austin Ranney makes a strong argument against the system as
a whole:

The primary system freed forces driving toward the disintegration of party organizations and facilitated the construction of factions and cliques attached to the ambitions of individual leaders. The convention system compelled leaders to treat, to deal, to allocate nominations. . . . Indeed, the fact that aspirants for nomination [in a primary system] must cultivate the rank and file makes it difficult to maintain an organizational core dedicated to the party as such; instead, leadership energies operate to construct activist clusters devoted to the interests of particular individuals.[15]

Nonpartisan Elections.   Perhaps the broadest attack on the parties was the call for nonpartisan elections at the local level. This not only kept the rascals out of selecting local leaders, it kept them out of the game altogether. Nonpartisanship was a Progressive concept of the first order because it reflected both the desire to eliminate evil and the urge to benefit from the efficiency and economy of the new age of management. City managers, who were expected to be above partisan concern and professional in their training and outlook, were coincidental with the spread of nonpartisanship. Budget reforms, city commissions, and a host of civil service reforms were also part of the Progressive package. Whatever the ultimate objectives, the first step was, in Brookings Institute Scholar James Sundquist's words, "a seizure of political and governmental power by those in favor of change. . . . reform required dethroning the political bosses who, in alliance with the holders of concentrated economic power, defended the status quo."[16]

Although most of the Progressive efforts were initially seen in the Midwest and West, one of the first major cities to become nonpartisan was Boston. In 1909, under the control of the Yankee-dominated state legislature, the city electoral system was changed in an attempt to stem the influence of the Irish. The Boston Finance Commission was established at the same time as a committee of civic-minded Brahmins appointed by the governor to watch over the city's fiscal behavior. Having lost control of the parties and the government, the old guard moved into such civic watchdog or do-good organizations, and tried to limit the political power of their opposition. It was a bitter fight and although part of the focus of the reform was to extend the franchise, there was also the darker desire to preserve the system for the more established class.[17]

Taking the parties out of the contest for office at the local and county levels of government across the nation did not eliminate politics, but it did have a substantial effect on the function of the parties at those levels, and indirectly, on the nature of the party system as a whole. Not contesting office at those levels eliminated the main reason for the local party's existence. The city and county parties could still participate in elections for state legislatures, governor, or federal office, but the rewards at the state and national levels tend to be more abstract and less of an incentive for active local party membership.

There has been relatively little attention paid by political scientists to the consequences of nonpartisan elections, but what research there is suggests that Republicans appear to have done better than Democrats because they are more likely to dominate the civic associations, which are the only organizations left at the community level when the parties are eliminated. Presumably, this finding is truer of smaller and middle-sized cities than the large urban metropolises where ethnic identifications are apt to function as cues to large numbers of voters. The 1910 election in Boston, for instance, brought John F. "Honey Fitz" Fitzgerald, the grandfather of John F. Kennedy, into office.

The assumption is that the old-boy network decides whom it wants to support, and since there is little countervailing effort on the part of opposing organizations—because there are no effective opposing organizations—their candidate wins. The scenario is based on sociological evidence about organizations: those who tend to join them and rise to leadership levels are more likely to be middle and upper middle-class persons who are demographically identical with the typical Republican party member. At the voting level, without the impetus of the party machinery to get out the vote of the more-typically Democratic working-class voter, those who participate in nonpartisan elections are also likely to be the better educated, higher-class Republican voters.[18] The benefit to Republicans is probably also enhanced by the tendency of such nonpartisan elections to be held in off years or as single races which do not combine with the partisan election for state or national office. The limit to Republican domination is that it has been the minority party since the 1930s and there just are not enough of them to dominate every organization in every town.

In many cities across the nation, the factions that form to support candidates for office can change from year to year, leaving the voters in doubt about whom they are voting into office and whom they are voting out. The names of organizations are not necessarily misleading, but neither are they especially informative: in Cambridge, Massachusetts, the "Independents" are the old guard, while those more typically associated with political reform are known as the Cambridge Civic Association. And since much of Cambridge's media is dominated by Boston, the choice is not always clear. However vague we may feel the two major parties are, we do have a sense about the kinds of people likely to be elected when we make a choice based on a party label.

There do not appear to be definitive statistics on the subject, but it is estimated that at least half of the elected officials in the nation attain their positions through nonpartisan elections.[19] Whatever the expectations of the Progressive reformers may have been, the net effect for the party system has been a serious decline in relevance of the parties when those offices are sought. Even though the statistics may suggest a Republican gain, the party itself does not necessarily feel it or benefit from it because office holders elected on their own owe little or nothing to the party and are not likely to deal with it at all unless and until they seek higher office.

Nonpartisan office holders can also be constrained from establishing strong party ties, even when they want to, because of the need they feel to be nonpartisan. The political prospects of several mayors in Kansas City are a case in point. In a 1980 editorial in *The Kansas City Times,* the writer reviewed the history with regret.

During the glory years of former Mayor Ilus W. Davis (1963–1971), there were those who predicted a bright political future for him based on his municipal record. Ike Davis happened to be a Democrat, but as a non-partisan mayor he had no inclination and few opportunities to foster a personal base here or across Missouri. Mayor Charles B. Wheeler, who served from 1971–1979, learned the lesson the hard way when he campaigned for higher office while still at City Hall. The votes and the alliances were not there. . . . By accepting the non-partisan role, any mayor cuts himself off from the lifeblood of the political precincts.[20]

Whether the precincts are there or not, the kinds of organizational backing it takes to win a nonpartisan election draws from the activities that sustain party precincts. For most, it also takes the support required to sustain them.

Decline Through External Factors

The reforms went a long way toward weakening the parties in America, but they were not the only cause of party decline. There were reforms in other areas, such as the spread of civil service regulations, which were intended to have some impact on the parties, but actually aimed more at government itself. There were historic events that shaped our attitudes toward all institutions, such as the Vietnam War and Watergate. And there were more subtle social changes in the fabric of American society, such as the women's movement and the communications revolution.

CIVIL SERVICE REFORM

The capacity to offer a job or a contract has been a major incentive in party growth and maintenance since the time of Andrew Jackson. It is, in political science terms, a "material" incentive: "tangible rewards: money, or things and services readily priced in monetary terms."[21] Incentives are what motivate persons to participate in organizations. We will address two other kinds of incentives ("solidary," which refers to the sociability that comes from participation and "purposive," which refers to the purpose, or ideal which an organization may serve) later in this chapter, but at this point it is important to note that the immediate material reward of a job or a contract, upon which all local political machines were based, was directly challenged when government jobs were protected from electoral changes, and contracts were required by law to be offered to the lowest bidder.

An interesting modern application of patronage that reflects the nature of our political life is the hiring of law firms to supplement the work of government. Contracts to lawyers are not typically handled by bids and it has become one of the few areas of spending to be unaffected by decades of civil service reform. A comment reported in *The Washington Post* undoubtedly reflects the patronage approach: "The people who fund government,—i.e., the campaign contributors—should be given preference when it comes to awarding legal work."[22]

We are not arguing the moral implications of the civil service reform, but only noting that as it grew, beginning with the Pendleton Act of 1893 in Congress, it cost the party, particularly the local parties, one of the most important rewards it could offer at the ward and city levels. Patronage was a form of upward mobility to many immigrant groups in urban ghettos. If some could get jobs in return for getting out the vote of their neighbors, they would strive for a large turnout. Votes, after all, are easy to measure, so party bosses were in a good position to judge the effectiveness of their minions and offer rewards accordingly.

The civil service reforms were part of the "economy and efficiency" theme of the Progressive movement. They were designed to bring a sense of professionalism to government work, and equally important, they were intended to limit the capacity of party bosses to hire their minions or fire the workers of their predecessors. While never entirely freeing the public work force from the influence of electoral outcomes, they have provided substantial security for many and proved to be a hinderance to the party's capacity to use jobs as a material incentive for participation.

THE NEW DEAL

Franklin D. Roosevelt forged a major realignment in 1934, with the creation of a new coalition for the Democratic party that made it the major party in the United States. At the same time, however, he seriously undercut the organizational strength of the local party machines by eliminating or reducing the dependence of the urban poor on the party for its welfare in times of trouble.

Until the New Deal, government, especially the national government, did little to intervene on behalf of its citizens. It collected taxes and tariffs (as a protection for politically important business interests). It built roads and maintained the postal service. It provided for the national defense (growing considerably during World War I) and some public health services. After the Progressive Era, it intervened to regulate the activities of large industrial interests, but on the whole it did not concern itself with whether its citizens were clothed or housed, or especially well fed. These latter tasks fell to the private interests: churches, civic and other charitable groups, and the local political parties which would provide the necessary benefits when it could or intervene on behalf of its members with other organizations or government agencies when that was appropriate.

The local party was part of the neighborhood. Its members spoke the same language and came from the same background as those it helped. As one Irish-American citizen noted not too long ago, "You grew up in Boston knowing your ward and your parish."[23] Social security, and the myriad of programs that have come from the government since the beginning of the New Deal took the party out of the business of providing almost all such services. The single remaining activity left to the local party was—and is—its role as a mediator between the party faithful and the government. It is a role much circumscribed, however, in the cities and counties where nonpartisan elections hold sway and where office holders have established "little city halls" or local congressional offices to handle the case work of their constituents.

UPWARD MOBILITY

The political parties were not immediately affected by the cutoff in immigration by Congress in the 1920s because the machines were still populated by a generation of immigrants whose need for assistance and habits of political behavior were not likely to change even with the social programs of the New Deal. With the end of World War II, however, the situation changed as the children of immigrants—with the help of the G.I. Bill—attained higher levels of education and moved up the socioeconomic ladder to the suburbs.

In the 1950s and early 1960s, politics became populated by what Harvard political scientist, James Q. Wilson called the "amateur democrats," persons with a more cosmopolitan view of politics, who see it as being about ideas and principles rather than people, who participate because it is their civic responsibility to do so, not because of the immediate or material reward it will bring them.[24]

One rear guard battle that probably marked the turning point between the regulars and the amateurs in New York City took place in 1965, when an alliance was formed between Robert F. Kennedy and the reform clubs in the city. The year before, when Kennedy ran for the Senate, he was brought in and supported by the regulars and opposed by the reformers. An alliance was struck over a surrogate court judgeship, and Kennedy (although out of the country during most of the campaign) brought all of his considerable resources to the race: the campaign staff was made up of the same people who had managed the Senate race. On the day of the primary, a busload of sixty-five workers from the farm club in Boston came down to "help out at the polls." The "help" included suggesting to those standing in line in the precincts controlled by the regulars that they should be prepared to be fingerprinted, or having a photographer wander up and down the line snapping pictures. It was politics of the old school—before Watergate gave "dirty tricks" a bad name—but in retrospect, the campaign marked the passage of power from one generation and one style of politics to the next.

The amateurs were well educated, typically lawyers, academics, and college-educated housewives. Although originally drawn to the reform movement because of their dedication to issues and the larger good, they stayed because they enjoyed the camaraderie of like-minded people. In cities such as New York, membership in the local reform club replaced the church or country club, where single and recently-married couples might make friends or find potential mates. It was often said that New York's Lexington Club had the largest membership because its president, Russ Hemenway, was an especially attractive eligible bachelor who attracted interested women, who in turn attracted interested men. The importance of incentives should never be underestimated.

The new generation was not so much afraid of power as disdainful of those who exercised it within the parties. In the Republican party, activists in the West revolted against the domination by the eastern establishment. It was the core of the Goldwater support that first materialized in 1964, and has influenced Republican party politics ever since. In the Democratic party, amateurs fought professionals over control of the machines in cities, such as Chicago and New York, and for control of the issues in California where the party structure never had been strong. The old guard gradually lost ground because they could no longer provide the rewards they once did, and because many of their earlier followers found other sources of support, or no longer needed the kind of help the party had been accustomed to giving.

Without a material incentive to offer, the new party leaders substituted the solidary reward of social enjoyment. The enemy was clear, and the meetings were fun. The young activists of the 1950s and early 1960s were confident in their ability to win. It was, like the Progressive Era, a time of affluence and high expectation. And, like the Progressive Era, the object of change was the betterment of government, greater democracy, and the elimination of the political bosses.[25]

The elimination of poverty and social injustice, while perhaps given lip service by the reformers, did not appear to be high on their list of priorities. Adlai Stevenson and later John F. Kennedy were the national models. At the local level, objectives varied from eliminating the old-line bosses to promoting liberalism. The liberal reformers in such cities as New York, however, could not really differentiate their policy positions from their opponents because the regulars were equally liberal and, in some cases, more so.

The difference was between reform and liberalism. Although the distinctions are not difficult to discern (the former tends to refer to processes of governance, and the latter to social policies), there has always been a blurring of the two in the popular use of the terms. To some it came down to a question of priorities: if the processes were honest and open, then the social benefits would naturally follow. To others, the power of the bosses assured them that the people who needed social services would be seen to because the bosses needed their support. Wilson makes the point that the two are related in one important way: "It is another way of stating the amateur conviction that the ends of government ought to provide the motivation for undertaking political action. . . . the party must be 'genuinely' liberal—i.e., it must profess liberalism out of conviction rather than expediency."[26]

For the party system, the revolution of conservatives in the Republican party and liberals in the Democratic party was a revolution of generations. The coming to power of a new generation was important for the durability of the system, but it was not enough. Having defeated the enemy in both parties, the new leaders found themselves with a different set of problems and difficulty coming together to solve them.

DECLINE IN CONFIDENCE IN ALL INSTITUTIONS

In the late 1960s and early 1970s, there was widespread loss of confidence in all institutions by Americans. According to political scientists Seymour Martin Lipset of Stanford and William Schneider of the American Enterprise Institute, the loss of faith was not focused on politicians or big business as had been characteristic of previous eras of crisis, but all public and private institutions at the same time.[27] It was a time of marked civic unrest and great social changes. It was also the time when political observers were most certain that the parties were moribund institutions, incapable of handling the conflicts tearing the nation apart. The certain optimism that characterized the reformers of previous generations disappeared. The assassinations and urban riots of the 1960s, Vietnam, and Watergate had combined to cast doubt on the institutions. Normally, reformers believe in the institutions but doubt the intentions of those who run them; or alternatively, they believe in the need to pit one large institution against another (for example, government against business). By the mid-1970s, faith had declined all around, and among those still willing to try, the issue was whether one worked for change within the institutions, or whether it was better to withdraw entirely and seek their destruction by ignoring them or overthrowing them.

Curiously, those who remained strong party identifiers were also those with the greatest faith in the system, but it is not clear which way the linkage runs: Are those who have faith in the parties more likely to have faith in all institutions? Or is confidence of political, rather than psychological or sociological origin, in which case decline in partisanship would lead to a decline of faith in all other institutions?[28] Either way, pollsters continuously reported a decline in partisanship among the American electorate, and political observers repeatedly eulogized the death of the parties.

The loss of faith should be put in some perspective, however. For one thing, the parties were weak. They were actively weakened by several generations of reformers and by the intergenerational conflict between the amateurs and regulars in the 1950s and early 1960s. Organizationally, they were circumscribed by state laws in determining how they could be structured and, in many instances, how their leaders were to be chosen. Nonpartisan elections had cost the party almost complete control of the nomination in the remaining offices. And beyond all that, the nation was beset with strong, difficult conflicts centering around basic questions of civil rights, justice, war and peace, and later economic direction. The parties had positions; they did not appear to have answers.

The conflicts in the society were reflected within the parties as those espousing competing values fought for control of one of the few remaining vehicles open to control. Although we will discuss the role and impact of the party reforms of the period in the next chapter, the fact that the parties (particularly the Democratic party) appeared to be torn apart by dissention added to the common view that they were in disarray and in no position to bring peace. The Great Society programs of Lyndon Johnson had carried the Democratic party farther to the left, raising the hopes and expectation of many of those who felt disenfranchised and creating conflict with those who were threatened by movement in the lower classes, especially among those in the working class just one rung up the ladder. Liberal Republicans, such as Nelson Rockefeller and George Romney, who accepted the role of government responsibility developed in the New Deal, were challenged by conservatives identified with Goldwater and Reagan (Reagan called them "bright" colored Republicans, compared to the "pastel" shades of the Republican New Dealers). Richard Nixon kept the allegiance of one group and dealt with the other in the years of his presidency. The conflicts in both parties simmered, sometimes they boiled over, but at best the parties were only the battlefield; they were in no position to end the war.

Trouble within the parties was reflected by the growth of special interest organizations outside the parties. No one seemed to need the parties: candidates created their own organizations to win election; interests supported their own organizations to lobby government and influence public opinion. And voters—that best of all gauge of party strength—split their ballots in increasing numbers, when they bothered to vote at all.

Many decried the weakness of the parties, and most were pessimistic about their potential for regeneration:

> But today it is not just these minority-group "outsiders" who are frustrated by the inequalities of our society and the laggard performance of our political-governmental system. Millions of middle-aged, white working Americans are coming to understand that they have been victimized by the irresponsible politics of the recent era. . . .
> I am not optimistic about the prospects of reviving responsible party government in the near future. The momentum of current trends, the drift of the public mood seem to me to point in the opposite direction: toward the further fracturing of the already enfeebled party structure in this decade. . . . That habit of partisanship, once lost, may be very difficult to regain. If that proves to be the case, and if the young people entering the electorate remain independent of the party system as they now appear to be, the major parties may no longer enjoy a monopoly of high office. . . .
> If the distrust of politicians and parties continues to grow, it may be reflected in the deliberate crippling of responsible leadership, by dividing the branches of government between the parties and by turning officeholders out as soon as they show signs of amassing any significant power.[29]

SOCIAL CHANGES

The 1960s and 1970s were marked by the emergence of mass movements, but perhaps the most significant movement of all was the women's movement, because it altered not only the policy agenda but, more critically, it changed the way women participate in politics and the way men and women lead their lives. Prior to the women's movement, women were the mainstay of volunteer activity, particularly as low-level workers in campaigns. Despite the differences in the professional strength of the two major parties at the national level, most local party activity in both parties is based on volunteers. The lowered economy combined with the movement to send more women into the workforce, drying up a sizable portion of the volunteer pool, and those who continued to participate expected to so do at higher levels within the campaigns as managers and candidates themselves. The Republican party was particularly active in trying to recruit women as candidates following Watergate because of the image of honesty and integrity they project to the American voter. However, with the national party's rejection of the Equal Rights Amendment and the Democratic nomination of Geraldine Ferraro for vice-president, the GOP has been fighting an uphill battle to reach out to women voters.

Another aspect of the movement's impact was the change it made in the attitudes of both men and women about the quality of life: how they would prefer to spend their leisure time; greater devotion to health care and exercise as opposed to social but less athletic endeavors. The "me" generation of the 1970s was actually a generation, or at least a decade, devoted to private pursuits at the obvious cost to public activity. The solidary rewards that had played such an important role among the reformers of the 1950s were less attractive, because social benefits could be found elsewhere—at the health club, in other sports activities—in a host of alternative settings developed in response to an increased portion of the population living alone.

Another aspect of the more isolated living conditions was an increase in the fear of crime, an issue that more often than not headed the list of priorities respondents offered to pollsters. Canvassing one's neighbors became a rather tricky business as people became strangers to each other. One hesitated to knock on an unknown door; one hesitated to open the door to an unknown knocker.

The media that informed has also always entertained. When the single individual or nuclear family was not out in pursuit of better health, he, she, or they could be found at home watching television in any of its many forms from cable to video tapes. This home entertainment has taken its toll on the community activities that politics requires. While the incentives to remain at home have increased, the incentives to host large-scale political events decreased because of the danger that they might fail to attract a crowd, which would be bound to be reported in the media. With the advent of complex campaign finance legislation at the federal level, the absolute confusion, in the early years particularly, in allocating income and expenditures for such events and the need to centralize activities for reporting purposes have also been factors in discouraging local political party activities.

Why People Become Party Activists: The Changing Incentives for Participation

The first responsibility of any organization is to maintain itself. If the party cannot maintain the active participation of its volunteer base because the old rewards were no longer available, or no longer sufficient as incentives, it behooves it to offer alternative rewards.

This is an especially difficult problem for party leaders (compared to leaders of other kinds of organizations) because there are so many external constraints imposed on their behavior by the law as well as by changes in society. The material incentives, which once maintained the local organizations and contributed to the decentralized nature of the party system, have all but been eliminated. Even the solidary incentives of labor-intensive campaign activities have been affected by the technology, the need for centralization, and the limits on campaign expenditures. Volunteers are still sometimes employed to do the envelope stuffing, but it does not seem to be the same route up the campaign ladder that it used to be because each step, each activity, is directed by paid professionals. There is a choice now between using volunteers and using professionals, and it lessens the importance of the volunteer role.

What remains to the party are purposive incentives, defined by James Q. Wilson as an "intangible reward that derives from the sense of satisfaction of having contributed to the attainment of worthwhile causes."[30] In contrast to the older rewards of upward mobility, contacts, and the camaraderie of stuffing envelopes, that sustained the local organizations and helped maintain the decentralized nature of the party system, purposive rewards work best at the national level. Issues can divide as well as unite people, but they are more likely to be divisive at the local level. One person's ideal is invariably another's *bête noire*. When the kinds of issues that are raised are capable of sustaining strong commitments, or at least commitments strong enough to get individuals out of their homes and into party politics, they are also likely to alienate others and the cleavage may be more than a local organization can tolerate if they are local issues. This is all the more likely since positions that are apt to evoke strong commitments usually come only for those positions held by minorities. Persons holding the majority view rarely feel sufficiently threatened to get riled up about it.

Writing in 1973, Professor James Q. Wilson suggested that, given the increased levels of education in the society and the impact of the media, "it is possible the purpose and principle have increased in importance as political incentives."[31] Since then, the technological shift to direct mail solicitations for fund raising and political education has come to dominate much of American politics at the national level and has more than proven the point since these appeals are based entirely on purposive incentives.

DO THE INCENTIVES MATTER?

Throughout, we have considered the motivation for most of the reforms of the party system to be based on fear of undue influence—on the abuse of power. Typically, we assume that abuse is based on a material incentive, that is, the use of public power for private benefit. Solidary incentives are no threat to society, but they require an organization based on them to avoid controversy to some extent, lest it threaten the sense of camaraderie. When the material rewards were seriously curtailed for the parties from without, local parties and campaigns often sustained themselves on the solidary rewards and on the transient issues of each campaign. But even the solidary benefits have become less attractive due to changes in lifestyle.

The problem of incentives raises the interesting question of purpose and what the parties are all about. In the 1940s, the American Political Science Association took the rather controversial position that the parties ought to be responsible, that is they ought to stand for something beyond the opportunity to throw the rascals in power out of power. The ensuing debate defined the parties down to the reduced expectation that they existed solely for the purpose of contesting elections. As a function, however, contesting elections has failed to sustain party strength.

Professor Wilson was right: the only remaining incentive is purposive, and it is best offered at the national level. The debunked position of those who argued forty years ago that the parties must take stronger positions on issues may turn out to be right in the long run. Assuming they do, then the party system will change accordingly. It is our thesis that the change has already occurred, and what remains to be seen is how much ideology the two-party system can tolerate without losing its capacity to remain consensual.

The question also remains of how the party develops its principles. The Democrats have a notable history of trying to develop their positions in issue conventions and other highly visible forums of debate, which do not seem to work well. Those who participate tend to be more committed than the party proper. The Republicans have developed their stands in quieter circumstances, but both parties have been most successful reaching beyond their core support, when the voters come to accept the programs of the president —after he has proven that they work. The last great realignment occurred in 1934, after Roosevelt had a chance to set the New Deal in motion. The rise in Republican registration in 1984 may have been an acknowledgment that Reagan was successful in bringing down inflation and getting the economy moving again.[32]

Conclusion

Throughout our history we have held rather ambivalent attitudes toward the party system. Part of the ambivalence is probably psychological: we like our friends and like to think of ourselves as standing up for our principles. In truth, we only tolerate others standing up for theirs. Part of our desire to control the parties reflects an expectation of liberty and concern for anything that might limit it. Rarely have our expectations included the belief that the parties play a critical role in the functioning of democracy. And rarely have we been able to find a stable balance in adjusting the relationships of power.

The reform of the caucus system set in motion the development of a national party structure with formal ties to the state and local parties. It also set the expectation that the parties would have a formal decision-making process open to more than an inner clique. The Progressive reforms moved further from the expectations of the Founding Fathers and extended the "franchise" downward to the average, not just the "distinguished," citizens of the state. Throughout, the unstated assumption has been that the party leaders should not influence the choice of the nominee, that the presidential candidates, particularly, ought to be selected democratically, that is, elected to nomination. In the process of limiting that influence, the reforms also weakened the organization to the point where it was incapable of self-determination. While we maintained a number of positive feelings toward the parties, we also made participation in them as unappealing as possible.

The decline of the parties was a gradual process. The reforms struck at the abuse of power but they hit the capacity of the organization to sustain itself in a changing world. The parties reached their nadir when a new generation grew up that did not have a history of commitment (because of jobs or ideological ferver, or even habit), and when the organizations were too weak to offer new incentives because they had so little control over their own processes. The loss of control of the nomination was the most critical. It left the parties in a passive position. The candidates were self-selected and represented what they, or their ad agencies, wanted them to represent. Robert Redford's portrayal of *The Candidate* in the early 1970s was a good composite of what we thought our candidates were. The Kennedy style (the windblown hair, the restrained energy) was what political consultants looked for, and often what they found for us. The choices offered in elections were between individuals or ad-hoc coalitions of interest groups. It seemed as if that would be the waive of the future until the campaign finance law intervened to limit the interests and make infinitely more complicated the job of running for office. As usual, no one anticipated the outcome of the reform, but surprisingly, it worked to the benefit of the parties.

PART
II

THE NEW PARTY STRUCTURE

The Democratic National Committee Meets to Consider a New Party Symbol

(ARNOLD ROTH)

Back from the Depths:
Party Resurgence

THE POLITICAL PARTIES in America reached a crisis in the late 1960s and early 1970s. It was then that political pressure tore at the traditional coalition of the Democratic party. It was then that Watergate cast such a pall on the Republican party. It was then that David Broder wrote *The Party's Over.*[1] He was not alone in describing the desperate straits into which the parties had fallen. Every election seemed to bring more evidence of party decline. Every reform effort on the part of the Democrats seemed to lead the party into a further morass of confusion and hostility.

In this chapter we will describe what happened then and how both parties addressed the crises before them. We will explain what the parties do—how that vague machinery operates in American political life—and what steps have been taken to make the parties more than they have been before. It is our view that the party system emerging in the 1980s is different than what existed before: it performs more functions than we have been accustomed to expect from the parties, and in order to perform those functions, it has dramatically increased its tasks and its leadership role.

Most of our description will be about the activities of the Republican party because it is further along in organizational development, but the party resurgence is due to the efforts of both parties. The Democratic reforms, while painful at the time, were consistent with the needs of the organization to adjust itself to a changing environment and play an important role in the developing strength of the system as a whole. The activities within both parties did not go unnoticed by the other and so, while each focused on a separate problem, both benefited by the solutions found to the other's search: the Republicans became more sensitive to participation, and the Democrats began to develop different expectations about the relationship between the party and its candidates.

The Democratic Reforms

Political parties are rarely staid organizations flowing smoothly from election to election. They are, after all, contesting for power and seek to benefit from the political divisions within the society. The Democrats have been more fractious than the Republicans because they are the majority party (and hence have more to fight over), and because they are composed of a coalition of groups within the population that do not necessarily share the same values and expectations. The changes the Democrats made reflected their coalitional base and the need the party had to respond equitably to groups seeking influence. The changes were directed at the core of the national party's traditional function: the selection of the presidential nominee.

THE HISTORY

The first strains, which appeared in the 1950s, were over questions of civil rights. Black and white liberals expected more because of the New Deal hopes of a better life and because of the horrors of the war, which revealed the consequences of intolerance. On the other hand, part of the coalition was drawn from conservative whites in the South who valued their supremacy and their states' right to determine their own course. The battle lines within the party were drawn on questions of qualification for the national committee and the presidential nominating convention. It reached the boiling point in 1968, when the entire Mississippi delegation and half the Georgia delegation were refused their seats at the Democratic national convention because the state parties had violated a four-year-old rule against racial discrimination.[2]

Also, 1968 was the year in which the peace movement was added to the turmoil of the civil rights movement and the lines were drawn for a major cleavage within the party. The assassinations of Martin Luther King, Jr., and Robert F. Kennedy added to the despair of many who had hoped for resolution within the party, and the division within the convention hall and the nation were reflected in the riots in the streets of Chicago. Losing the election that year forced the Democratic party to take a serious look at itself, and it began the cumbersome process of reform by creating a series of commissions, which met between the conventions and were answerable to the national committee.

THE DEMOCRATIC COMMISSIONS

There were four formal commissions between 1968 and 1982, all designed to develop rules for selecting delegates to the national presidential nominating convention (a fifth commission dealt with the convention itself). It may be one of the ironies of political life that the national party should have succeeded in altering the flow of influence and the structure of the system on the one issue in which it has all of the responsibility and almost none of the control.

During the 1968 primary period, Connecticut supporters of Senator Eugene McCarthy recognized there were no rules to prevent the strong regular party forces from giving them a fair share of representation in the state delegation to the national convention. The McCarthy campaign formed an Ad Hoc Commission on Democratic Selection of Presidential Nominees, chaired by Governor Harold Hughes of Iowa. The commission report concluded that neither the system of selecting delegates by the states, nor the procedures of the convention itself were in keeping with democratic principles and proposed a number of reforms which came in time to form the basis of the party-authorized McGovern-Fraser Commission.

A major theme of the Ad Hoc Commission was the need to include more people in the decision-making process. It was a theme that would be repeated in the next several years, and although it created a great deal of controversy, it led to the inclusion of many more women, blacks, Hispanics, and other minorities within the mainstream of the party.

McGovern-Fraser.   After the 1968 election, Senator Fred Harris of Oklahoma, with the support of Hubert Humphrey, was chosen as the new chairman of the Democratic National Committee (DNC). Harris, in turn, chose Senator George McGovern of South Dakota to chair a study of the 1968 presidential nominating process, the report of the Ad Hoc Commission, and make recommendations for the future. When McGovern resigned in order to run for the presidency, Representative Don Fraser of Minnesota was appointed to take his place.

According to Byron Shafer, a political scientist at the Russell Sage Foundation, the commission Harris put together amounted in the end to a replacement of the party regulars with the party reformers, some of whom had come from the reform movement of the 1950s, but most of whom came from the candidacies and issues of the 1968 presidential campaign. The recommendations of the Commission on Party Structure and Delegate Selection led to one of the most far-reaching reforms in American party politics ever instituted from the inside.[3]

At the structural level, the commission called for the codification of national standards to govern state and local parties. This was a sharp departure from the American experience of party "stratarchy," with little influence exercised from one level of party structure to another, and what leverage there was, going from the local to the national, not the other way around. From the very beginning, the focus was on participation in the process, and beyond that, on the inclusion of specific groups which were traditionally underrepresented in the party and in the decision making of society as a whole. Among the specific recommendations were the following:

- requiring representation of women, young people, and minorities in reasonable relationship to their presence in the state's population;
- requiring delegate candidates to identify their presidential choices;
- prohibiting a presidential candidate or a party leader from naming individuals who would make up the slate of delegates, whether pledged to a candidate or not;
- prohibiting ex-officio delegates;
- requiring each step in the delegate selection process to begin in the calendar year of the convention;
- limiting party committee selection of the delegates to 10 percent of the total delegation.[4]

The McGovern-Fraser Commission had a dramatic effect on the presidential selection process in particular and on the make-up of party activists in general, but other factors contributed in a major way to the overall changes in American presidential politics in the years to follow: the increase in the number of state primaries and caucuses (fostered in part by the reforms, and in part by the economic incentives and media attention such events generate); changes in federal campaign finance law, which placed an emphasis on small donations and centralized campaign organizations; and the technology of raising money and running for office. In 1972, however, when the reforms were put into practice, they were extraordinarily controversial and costly to the electoral coalition that constituted the base of the Democratic party. Many of the old guard, particularly organized labor, were hostile to George McGovern and his followers and deserted the party by the tens of thousands.

The Mikulski Commission. After the 1972 campaign, a new commission was created by the Democratic party to refine the reforms of the McGovern-Fraser Commission. It was led by Barbara Mikulski, a Maryland party leader who was later elected to Congress from Baltimore.

The Mikulski Commission relaxed some of the new requirements and was less hostile to party involvement. It allowed the state committees to select 25 percent of their delegation to the national convention, and eliminated the rule that committee members identify their presidential preferences. It also abolished winner-take-all primaries and encouraged proportional representation in caucuses and conventions in an effort to keep relatively strong candidates in the running who might not have done well in early primaries (a reform that seemed less controversial when the party did not have an incumbent president running for re-election).

The Winograd Commission. Following the 1976 campaign, a third commission, named after its leader, Michigan state party chairman Morely Winograd, was established to continue refining the rules in the face of accrued electoral experience.

Whereas the 25 percent at-large portion of the state's delegation under Mikulski was designed to assure affirmative action goals, the Winograd Commission added another 10 percent to the delegation for party and elected officials. It was the first recognition that the party establishment ought to have a role, and the Winograd Commission might have ended the reform cycle except for the election of Jimmy Carter who, having won under one system, did not want to see it changed. The recommendations of this commission were, therefore, largely ignored by the national party committee run by Carter supporters.[5]

The Hunt Commission. After Carter's defeat in 1980, yet another commission on delegate selection was created under the chairmanship of North Carolina Governor James B. Hunt. The charge of this commission was to do more than refine the process, it was to try to find a way to heal the wounds inflicted on the party by years of reform battles and the antiparty attitude of the defeated president. Included in the responsibilities were a review of a recent court decision that gave greater weight to the national party in defining state rules; analyses of the mixed caucus/primary system; consideration of the number and scheduling of caucuses and primaries with an eye toward shortening the prenomination season; review of affirmative action at all levels of party activity; and again, a look at the role of the party and elected officials in the nominating process, which this time appeared to be more concerned with finding a better way to choose a leader than guaranteeing a balance of representation in the process.[6]

Losing the White House was a fate to which reforming Democrats had grown accustomed since 1968; losing control of the Senate had a chastening impact. When the Hunt Commission met for the first time, party leaders were also recovering from four years of neglect if not outright hostility from the Carter presidency. There was a strong desire for rapprochement among the factions which fell prey along the way to the demands of supporters of the leading contenders for the next presidential race—a factor that colored all of the commissions. Winning the presidency, after all, is the best guarantee of getting one's views turned into policy, so designing the process to advance the interests of one candidate over another is an inevitable part of the effort.

A "balanced" commission, such as the Hunt Commission, is found when the Kennedy interests are matched equally against the Mondale interests. The process is considered unbalanced, or at least unfair, when another candidate comes along who might have done better under another arrangement of the rules. Both Jesse Jackson and Gary Hart had cause for complaint after the 1984 primary season, each of whom would have done better under another set of rules.

Among the major changes made by the Hunt Commission were a reorganization of the primary season, making it shorter, in the hope that it would be less likely to bore the American public; and expanding the size of the state delegation once again with the creation of "super delegates" representing the party leaders and elected officials in the continuing effort to tie the selection of the president to the party in the other branches of government.

The complaint was registered after the 1984 election that the super delegates abdicated their deliberative role by declaring their candidate preferences as soon as they were named to the position, instead of waiting until the convention to assess the relative merits of the candidates and back the strongest potential nominee. Both Gary Hart and Jesse Jackson complained that Mondale would not have had the nomination "sewed up" had the super delegates not behaved so. On the other hand, if the super delegates are selected because they represent the party proper—the mainstream of party workers—it would have been very surprising if they had chosen someone other than Walter Mondale who, more than any Demo-

cratic candidate running for the nomination in 1984, represented
the mainstream of the Democratic party.

Many of the reforms made by the various commissions did not
have the impact on the political process their advocates would have
wanted. Patrick Caddell, a leading political pollster, in a letter to
fellow members of the Hunt Commission written shortly before the
end of their work, made the following observations about the reform efforts:

> History instructs us on three points. One: Changes cannot be tallied in
> a vacuum, i.e., it is impossible to assess changes individually, each must
> be viewed in relation to all others and to the system as a whole. Two:
> Changes are not imposed on a static system, each change also alters the
> behavior and performance of the entire system, normally in ways
> severely underestimated at the time. Three: the goals sought by changes
> are often and regularly undone by consequences unanticipated and
> unplanned and thus reformers must always be vigilant and sensitive to
> such possible unintended consequences.[7]

Rick Stearns, a participant in all of the Democratic commissions, drew an interesting conclusion about the impact of the reforms on the relationship between the candidates and the party in
another memo to the Hunt Commission:

> Curiously, simultaneously with the consolidation of its grip on the
> nominating process, the national party has surrendered in equal mea-
> sure the actual power to enforce the purposes of its rules on the presi-
> dential candidates. While custom still requires the candidate to come
> to the convention in the guise of seeking its nomination, the candidate's
> role at the convention in fact is to enforce the rules that he or she has
> largely implemented. . . .
> While the rules have served these purposes as well as others (most
> notably, insuring that the composition of the convention conforms to
> an aggregate ideal), they are also the source of unanticipated frictions.
> The most important of these is the conflict generated between the state
> party and the candidate in the exercise of the add-on powers. . . . While
> these purport to be grants of power to the state parties, in fact considera-
> tions of affirmative action on fair reflection require that the selection of
> add-on delegates be managed by the candidate or his agent. A second
> source of friction lies in the obvious inconsistency between universal
> binding provisions, candidate vetting of delegates, and the theory of a
> deliberative convention. While a deliberative convention is theoretically

possible under present party rules (so long as no candidate enters the convention with a first ballot majority), the natural tendency of presidential candidates or their organizations to fill the ranks allotted to delegates with candidate loyalists, suggests instead that any second ballot deliberation would more likely be the result of negotiations among contending candidates than among delegates themselves. This result, of course, is no different from that achieved by the so-called "bossed conventions," simply fewer bosses participate in the brokering. A third source of potential friction may arise from among those who are the intended beneficiaries of the party's affirmative action rules. . . . It remains to be seen whether positions without power will long satisfy the proponents of aggregate reflection.[8]

In the decade and a half that the Democratic party sought to resolve the conflicts which so visibly beset it in 1968, it uncovered other problems. It tried excluding party regulars from the nominating process and it moved back and forth on the role of elected officials. It moved more surely toward the inclusion of those who had been underrepresented, but it tried toward the end to overcome the alienation of those who were threatened by affirmative action.

Whether or not the reforms succeeded in creating a system that will insure the selection of strong candidates, or whether they have succeeded in giving back to the national party the function of controlling the nomination of its presidential candidate, they have succeeded in making substantial changes in the make-up of Democratic party activists. Byron Shafer has called it a "quiet revolution," in which the elites "different in social background, political experience, and policy preference from the coalition which had previously dominated the national Democratic party" came to power.[9] It is a new generation—to be found in both parties—that others have described as "organizers," individuals concerned about the processes of change, who came out of the movements of the sixties, or at least out of that generation.[10]

Some might dispute Shafer's view that it was a "quiet" revolution, given the visibility in the press of the disputes within the party, but it was a revolution and it left the leadership of the Democratic party in a markedly different position in the 1980s than it had been in for some time. When Charles Manatt assumed the chairmanship of the party, after the defeat of Jimmy Carter, he

*The Republican National Committee Meets to Consider a New
Party Symbol*
(ARNOLD ROTH)

brought in talented people who stayed through the next four years (there had been almost 100 percent turnover in the first two years of the Carter presidency at the DNC) and began the process of building a stronger organization based on many of the techniques used in the Republican party. One small measure of his success was his ability to withstand Mondale's effort to unseat him in the 1984 convention.

The Republicans

While the Democrats focused their attention on organizational processes, the Republicans rebuilt their party with money and technology, although they, too, went through a major shift in political generations. Historically, the Republican party has always been better organized than its Democratic opponent. Some have attributed the stronger GOP structure to the inherent business nature of the party, others to the reliance Republican candidates have placed on the party for campaign support in contrast to the Democrats who have relied on labor to provide the organizational backbone of their campaigns thereby lessening the need for a strong party organization. The Republicans are also more homogeneous than Democrats and may, therefore, be more at ease relying on a permanent organization of like-minded people than Democrats who structure both the party and their campaigns on the basis of the separate constituencies which make up the party. The Democratic structure makes for an easy distribution of tasks, but a difficult process of communication which would weaken any organization.

The difference in focus between the two major parties appears to put the Republicans in a stronger position, but the reader should bear in mind that the contests between the parties are far more balanced than the relative party strength suggests. The Republican party outspends the Democratic party, but Democratic candidates typically outspend Republican candidates. In 1982, Democratic congressional candidates raised $91 million, compared to $85 million raised by their Republican opponents. Since much of the money is raised by incumbents who have relatively little need for it, the phenomenon of candidate political action committees (PACs) has emerged, providing a mechanism for members of Congress to support other members in the hope they will improve their internal struggles for leadership in the House or Senate or gain support for a presidential run. In addition, Democrats have non-monetary and nonreportable contributions available to them through labor and other membership organizations around the country which provide important volunteer help.

The question to be addressed in the long run is whether or not the new Republican organizational strength will make a substantial difference, and if it does, just what that difference will be.

THE HISTORY

The GOP has gone through two major periods of change since the 1950s—our base period. The party we see today is very much a product of those changes in substance and in process: the conservative revolt in 1964; and the post-Watergate era of rebuilding. We will describe the two periods in this section and reserve the specifics of party activities for the next section.

The 1964 Election.   The 1964 race for the presidency in which Barry Goldwater captured the nomination, but went down to defeat in a landslide to Lyndon Johnson, was in large part a challenge to the established leadership. It led to the same kind of transfer of leadership positions within the Republican party that Democrats were to experience a decade later. In the Republican case, western, middle-class activists replaced upper-class business and banking interests from the East. The schism was based more on geography and class than ideology, but it was fought out on an ideological ground. The resolution had to be found at the national level because of the distinct regional hostilities.

Following the election, Ray Bliss, a former state chairperson from Ohio, became the new chairperson of the Republican National Committee (RNC). Using the workers Goldwater brought into the party, Bliss began the process of rebuilding by focusing on national fund raising, local party structure, and a professional, full-time leadership at the top. Wary of the divisiveness on issues,

Bliss avoided policy positions by deferring to the Republican congressional delegation.

Beginning in 1965, the RNC began its direct mail fund raising program based on the Goldwater lists. Until then, the national committee had been funded by assessments made on the states—yet one more reason for state dominance of the national parties which has fallen away with the redirection of the flow of funds. By the time Rogers Morton succeeded Bliss, the finance committee responsible for raising state money had all but disappeared from the RNC structure.

It is more than likely that no one in the early years, including Bliss, understood the difference between the new generation of activists and the older one. James Q. Wilson published *The Amateur Democrat* in 1962, which was about a generational shift in the Democratic party, but the Republican shift came later and scholarship often takes awhile to become accepted in any case. The new generation of Republicans, like their Democratic counterparts, were motivated more by ideological considerations and less by expectations of the material rewards that had been important to their predecessors. Over time, it led both parties to greater cohesion on issues among the activists, but at a cost to the heterogeneity of the membership. At the time, the latter half of the 1960s, the shift at the local level occurred quite rapidly, although the national leadership was not completely aware of it. The value to the party was the tremendous support it was able to provide Richard Nixon's candidacy in 1968, helped even more by the disarray among the Democrats.

The Watergate Era. The second crisis faced by the Republican party is often calculated to have occurred in 1974 when the party tried to survive the scandals of Watergate and ended up losing forty-seven incumbents. In all likelihood, however, the position of the national party reached crisis proportions in 1972 when it was completely subordinated to the White House and the Committee to Re-Elect the President. Nixon's distance from the party was partly reflected in the re-election effort aimed at achieving 60 percent of the vote. In order to achieve their targeted vote count, they would have to attract a large number of Democrats and independents, and for that reason, none of the campaign material published by the Nixon-Agnew campaign carried the word "Republican" or the elephant symbol (a tactic that actually has been employed by both sides from time to time, depending on the popularity of the party or the party's presidential nominee).

The national party was also ordered by the president's people to stay out of the re-election bids of approximately three dozen Democratic congressmen who had been supportive of Nixon. Although these House elections may not have been winnable by the GOP, the party's lack of support for Republican opponents certainly contributed to the lack of any coattail effect in Nixon's victory, which was the most overwhelming since Johnson's election in 1964.

In a study undertaken for the RNC by polster Robert Teeter, he concluded that the Republican party bore a stronger resemblance to a minor party in the rest of the world than it did to a minority party in the American two-party system. That the GOP did not disappear entirely was, however, probably due to the two-party structure and the lack of an alternative. Most, if not all, of the Republican and conservative activists participating in politics since the Goldwater years had no place to go.

Mary Louise Smith became the RNC chairperson during the Ford presidency, and the party once again turned to rebuilding. Given the clear objective of winning back a respectable portion of voter support, there was an era of good feeling within the party until late in 1975 when Ronald Reagan announced his candidacy against President Ford. It may be that the division with the GOP in the contest for the presidency freed it from being entirely usurped by the presidential campaign of 1976, as it had been in 1972, and enabled it to address itself to other elections. For the first time, the national committee moved directly into campaigning to overcome the tremendous electoral losses of the 1974 elections.

Building on the efforts begun in 1964 to create a reasonably secure and loyal group of small donors, the RNC was probably the only party entity with a financial base, a surprising strength given the revelations about large donations to Nixon's re-election campaign and the subsequent Watergate scandals. In 1975, the RNC had approximately 300,000 on its mailing list, and the Congressional Committee had 25,000 (the Senate Committee had not yet moved to direct mail). With a gross budget of $9 million for the RNC in 1973–74, $4.5 to $5 million was directed into political activity at the congressional and gubernatorial levels. The Congressional Committee's budget was $2.3 million that year, which they cut to $1.7 million when only $200,000 had been raised in the first six months of the year.[11]

It may bear mentioning at this point that there is a major difference between Republican and Democratic party spending on behalf of their candidates. Republicans, in deference to their minority party standing, devote much of their resources to recruiting candidates and funding challengers. Democrats direct most of their resources to incumbents, not a surprising policy given the fact that it is the incumbent (not the party) who usually raises the money and does so because of his incumbency, and it is in the interest of the party to retain its numerical strength.

When William Brock succeeded Mary Louise Smith as chairperson, RNC attentions turned to state legislative as well as congressional races in preparation for the 1980 reapportionment. Although the effort was not notably successful in electoral outcomes (the Republican congressional candidates won 49.8 percent of the popular vote in the 1984 election, but picked up only 42 percent of the seats), it was an important departure for the national party and it generated and supported a cadre of professionally-trained, sophisticated campaign workers and candidates around the country. It was under Brock's leadership that the party made massive strides in income:

Republican Gross Income (In Millions)

1974	1975	1976	1977	1978	1979	1980
$6.3	$8.9	$19	$10.7	$14.5	$17	$37

SOURCE: From "Chairman's Report," 1978, 1979 (Washington, D.C.: Republican National Committee.

Throughout the latter half of the 1970s, 75 percent of the income came from direct mail solicitations, at a cost to the party that declined to 19 percent by 1980.[12] As the party regained strength, and especially as it became electorally competitive in the Senate and for the White House, its large donor program also increased from 198 $10,000 donors in 1978, to 865 such donors in 1980.

The spending disparities between the two parties grew significantly in the same period: In the 1977–78 electoral period, the Republicans spent $85.9 million compared to $26.9 million by the Democrats. In 1979–80, Republican spending increased to $161.8 million, to $35 million by Democrats, and in the 1981–82 election, the Republicans spent $213.9 million to $40 million by the Democrats.[13] Although, as we have already noted, party spending is not synomous with total election spending, and there was much more parity between the candidates, the dramatic surge in Republican fund raising was bound to have an effect on party's behavior and, possibly, on its strength in the long run.

The Changes

The financial growth of the Republican National Committee required decisions about what to do with the new resources, many of them made under Brock's tenure as RNC chairperson. Some of the new activities of the party were organizational in nature, such as the creation of issue task forces, which brought together representatives from the spectrum of Republican opinion and charged them with reaching a consensus. Some were technological. Not everything worked, but the party had the opportunity to learn from the experience. So, too, did the Democrats who emulated many of the Republican innovations as their candidates began calling for the same kinds of services Republican opponents were receiving. As Martin Schram noted in an article entitled "Why Can't the Democrats Be More like the Republicans? They're Trying," published in the *Washington Post* in the spring of 1982,

> One of Brock's first GOP creations was a program to attract young community leaders to Republicanism; he called it the "Concord Program." One of Manatt's first creations was a similar program for the Democrats. He called it the "Lexington Program."
> Today the Democrats are awash in Republican-style task forces and

targeting committees, strategy councils and study groups, programs for recruitment and programs for direct mail fund raising—and workshops where they tell each other how to put it all together.[14]

THE ORGANIZATIONAL CHANGES

Staffing. The focus on participation in campaigns was not a surprising reaction given the losses sustained by the Republican party in 1974. Under Brock, the party continued to direct its resources to campaigns instead of supporting local party organizations. Proven political professionals were hired to travel the states running seminars and offering advice. The National Committee paid for professional staff positions at the state level and tried employing regional directors, responsible for a group of states. Today, the regional directors have control over a wide array of resources with supporting staff in press, communications, and politics. There are now nearly a hundred people on the RNC staff with regional responsibilities.

When Brock's chairmanship ended with the Reagan election in 1980, he was succeeded by Dick Richards, who shifted the focus from campaign support to local party building, leaving most of the campaign work to the other two national Republican committees in the House and Senate. The growth of both of these committees has reached the stage where they are able to provide all of their candidates with the maximum amount of money allowed by the law, and an extraordinary array of campaign services which do not come under federal restrictions, such as advice on PAC fund raising, research, assistance in setting up direct mail and telephone bank services, polling data, and so on.

Issues. One departure in the rebuilding effort under Brock was to focus on issues through the use of task forces to develop a party agenda and the publication of a quarterly journal entitled *Common Sense,* which became a vehicle for developing and exploring Republican ideas. In time, the issue research done by the party almost completely replaced much of that function in Republican campaigns. The capacity of the party to maintain records on election districts and opponents, to do sophisticated voter analyses, and to develop and present policy positions would be hard for a campaign to match. The first step in research on any given topic for a campaign issue committee would be to contact the national party. It may not be a sufficient step for some campaigns, but it has become a building block.

The Republican task forces were a marked contrast in style from the Democratic issues conventions. What they may have lacked in visibility, they more than made up for in their capacity to build some measure of consensus. It is very hard, indeed, to reach a compromise with the public eye so finely focused and the constituencies back home so carefully attuned. The views developed by the party this way are not apt to meet the demands of its constituent members, but they do seem to suffice for the party.

Advertising.　Another departure for the national party, copied from the Conservative party in England, is what is known as "genre" advertising—media advertising that advocates the party and is not tied to a candidate. The low percentage of Republican identifiers in the post-Watergate years made such an effort especially appealing, and their ads have been among the most sophisticated and memorable in recent campaign advertising history.

The GOP began this institutional advertising in 1978, when the polls showed that any candidate for office labeled Republican started out 10 to 12 points behind in the polls automatically. The advertising campaign was designed to make Republicans feel better about being Republican, and to influence the large number of independents, particularly those in the baby boom generation, calculated to number about 75 million.

In 1980, the party spent $9 million with a series of ads running in four or five waves promoting the theme "Vote Republican. For a Change." The most effective ad depicted a Tip O'Neill look-alike in a large limousine running out of gas. The party credits the ads with an increase of 3 or 4 percentage points for their congressional candidates across the board.

In 1982, having won the White House and control of the Senate, the ads took a more defensive tone and urged voters to "Stay the Course." Again, the party credits the ads with keeping mid-term congressional losses down. The GOP lost twenty-six seats that year, instead of the forty-one or forty-two they expected to lose.

In the 1984 campaign, Mondale's pledge to raise taxes provided the theme for the party ads, and from late August on through the election, Republican party ads played on the prospect of increased taxes. The most successful ad in the series showed a group of people in an elevator with a Democratic congressman who was asked if he intended to support Mondale's tax plan. The party spent about $13 million on their genre advertising, expanding beyond television to radio and several *Reader's Digest* ads as well.[15]

Chairperson Brock noted in 1980, "There was a time just a few years ago when many people said there wasn't a dime's worth of difference between Republicans and Democrats. Our position on issues wasn't clearly defined, and most voters [who were angered or disappointed by the Republicans] felt that there was no real difference between the two parties."[16] The ads were designed to clarify the differences and to promote a positive attitude toward the GOP and a negative attitude toward the Democrats.

The Democratic party adopted the use of genre advertising as a counter measure, although it has not yet been able to put the funds into it that the three national Republican committees have to date. One Democratic ad played on a Republican ad from 1980. In the original Republican ad, a worker was shown talking about wanting a change. The Democratic follow-up showed the same worker saying that he had made a mistake and was speaking on behalf of the Democrats on his own, without getting paid for it.

Candidate Support in Primaries.   Under Brock, the Republican National Committee also began intervening in state primaries. It was a logical extension of the candidate recruitment program in which the party assured its prospect that it would provide as much support as possible. The national party entered into this area cautiously—and not always successfully, such as the time it supported a candidate for governor of Wisconsin who lost in the primary to Lee Sherman Dreyfus. Dreyfus went on to win the general election in 1978 and never did establish strong ties to the established Republican party. This departure into the primaries is a major step forward in recapturing control of one of a political party's most important functions: the control of its nominations.

Theoretically, it is possible for a national committee (more likely the House or Senate campaign committees) to support their own candidate, without regard to the partisan line-up in the state. It is not likely to be a common occurrence, but could, for instance, happen in a special election in the South where state law may call for a nonpartisan election.

In 1980, there was a party rules change—Rule 26 (f)—which limits the participation of the Republican National Committee to those instances approved by the state party chairperson and the national committee persons from the state. The congressional and Senate campaign committees are not affected by the limitations and continue to support candidates they believe to be most likely to win a general election. The Senate Campaign Committee, for instance, supported the moderate Elliot Richardson for the Senate nomination in Massachusetts in 1984, against a candidate who came out of the ranks of the more dominant conservative state party organization. Ray Shamie swamped Richardson in the primary election but ran far behind the Democratic nominee in the general election, as the national party committee would have predicted.

Primaries were designed to democratize the political process and eliminate the influence of party bosses as much as possible. Those who vote in primaries tend to be more active and committed party identifiers. Although federal law prohibits a party from behaving differently than a nonparty committee in primary contests for federal office (that is, for instance, contributing no more than $5,000), the legitimacy of party endorsement carries great weight among the party faithful. The nonmonetary contributions the party can make can be extensive, however. In the fall of 1983, the Republican Senatorial Committee sent out staff people to oversee the research, fund raising, polling, and telephone bank efforts in a special election in the state of Washington to fill the seat held by Senator Henry Jackson. The party also helped its candidate, former governor Dan Evans, get PAC funds.

On the odd occasion when the unendorsed candidate has won, it has meant some embarrassment and required some fence mending for the party establishment, but on the whole the intention has been to assure the strongest possible candidate for the GOP in those critical elections in which it has chosen to participate.

By 1978, 46 percent of the RNC expenditures were devoted to campaign support, divided equally between candidates for federal office and candidates for state and local office. Thirteen percent of the party resources were devoted to party development, and 12 percent to communications.[17] It was not until the 1980 election that the national party began to encourage grassroots participation by volunteers; until then the emphasis had been on professionalism and centrally-based decisions on whom to support and how to do it. The organization was designed to meet those objectives.

THE TECHNOLOGICAL CHANGES

The changes we would include in this discussion include the application of computer technology in fund raising, research, communications, and general campaigning; and the growing use of electronic media for training and communication with party activists and the electorate at large.

The Computerization of Politics. The extraordinary changes computers have made in American life have also been felt in politics in general and in the Republican party particularly because it has had the resources to invest in the new technology. By 1984, the congressional and the Senate campaign committees were so completely computerized that employees gave up writing memos and instead communicated with each other through the computer, whether in the office or on the road.

The benefits of electronic mail in campaigns can be profound. A staff member working in a campaign in a western state can, for instance, end the day with a campaign meeting at 9:00 in the evening, send in a report with questions and problems to the national office, and come into work the next day to find the questions answered because the Washington staff has had a three hour headstart on it.

Among the most important use of computers for the party itself has been the development of a series of sophisticated data processing systems, either based in Washington and made available to Republican state parties at low user rates, or through mini and personal computers. The programs provide for accounting and reporting, political targeting and survey processing, mailing list maintenance, donor preservation and information, and correspondence and word processing.[18]

Reaching the Voter. Perhaps the most important inroad of computerization is the capacity it provides for refining the communication that comes from the party. Messages can be targeted according to socioeconomic status, pulling the political and census geography together in a method called "digitizing." There are now three major firms with household lists (Donnelly, Metromail, and Polk) which include every household in the country with a listed telephone. The codes can identify households by specific census tracks or block groups and correlate them with relevant political information. The California Republican party, for example, is able to send out a mailing to all the residents in precincts that voted over 60 percent for Reagan in 1984, with an average age of over forty-five, in houses costing over $100,000, who have lived there for more than five years. Other state and some county parties are expected to gain that capacity in the next several years.

Until recently, there have been two kinds of lists used in direct mail solicitations: those bought from other sources (magazine, contributors to other causes, buyers of Ruby Red Grapefruit—the most "fruitful"—and other catalogs); and lists made up of party regulars. Mailing to lists of party registrants is usually a losing proposition unless the lists are correlated with other socioeconomic status (SES) data—a possibility existing only since the 1980 census. The capacity the technology provides to reach the right person with the right message opens tremendous possibilities in party communication.

In addition to fund raising, computers have also become powerful tools in communication for direct campaign activity. Historically, campaign lists came from church memberships, members of local organizations, and so forth, but each of the lists were ad hoc in nature and fairly expensive to manipulate on a reliable basis. The files now in process of being created will give the party a master list of over 500,000 voters in New Mexico, for example, which would be accessible by election districts for state representative. Such a list would include registered Democrats in the district who, when canvassed by telephone, said they would be willing to vote Republican, at least at the top of the ticket. King County, Washington has a refined list of voting behavior for 2,300 precincts.

Personal computers will carry the technological revolution even further—possibly even beyond the party because of the capacity of computer software firms to develop programs designed specifically for politics. By 1984, there were already fourteen firms selling software for personal computer campaigns. Although we think it is unlikely such firms will ever seriously challenge the capacity of the party to maintain the lists, that possibility does exist.

Direct Mail. Although the use of direct mail solicitations in politics is controversial because of its application by single issue groups and the new strength it has given them, it has come to play an important part of party building and maintenance since it was first used in the 1964 Goldwater campaign. The next successful use was by the Democrats in 1972 with the McGovern campaign, and it was not until a few years after that the Republican National Committee made it the linchpin of its fund raising strategy.

By 1978, the year the direct mail dividends really took off for the RNC, it had a base of 511,638 contributors, 58 percent of whom gave under $25.[19] In 1981, the first year of the Reagan administration, 77 percent of RNC funds came through the mail (with an additional 2 percent coming from telephone solicitations of those who had contributed through the mail in the past but had fallen off recently).[20] Of course, having the White House and the Senate also enabled the party to increase its large donor programs which amounted in 1981 to 20 percent total RNC income.[21] Still, the average contribution to the Republican party is under $30. In 1985, the party expects to be able to send mail to one out of every four households in the country.

Direct mail solicitations in American politics are generally based on negative appeals: urging the donor to return the envelope because he or she is angry about something. They are generally issue appeals, although issues can (and often do) include individuals, such as the RNC's successful appeal opposing Carter's U.N. Ambassador Andrew Young. Both parties (and a number of interest groups as well) made millions opposing and supporting Reagan's first Secretary of the Department of the Interior, James Watt. Party appeals seem to be most successful when they do not come in conflict with existing constituencies on the issues they are opposing: The RNC made money opposing the Panama Canal Treaty, the Democratic party did better opposing Reagan's proposed social security cuts than it did on environmental issues or the ERA (the fact that the social security appeal went out in a brown envelope bearing a strong resemblance to the mail which typically comes from the Social Security Administration was an interesting, albeit somewhat controversial, element in its success in the eyes of many direct mail specialists).

Because the Republicans now control both the administration and the Senate, the appeals require a certain amount of creativity to convince potential donors that there is a danger. In 1983, an airmail appeal was sent on the letterhead of the Hotel George V in Paris (mailed in England). The message was that the party leader sending the note could almost smell the tear gas as Parisians rose up in protest against the policies of the socialist government of François Mitterand. If Republicans were not vigilant enough, the same thing could happen in America.

The most successful appeals include something besides the dire warning. Appeals for a special purpose, such as enabling the party to mount a television advertising campaign usually work. A membership card to the party proper, or some special group within the party, is usually effective for both parties. The Republican Christmas card in 1984 included a smaller Christmas card to be mailed back to the Reagans (with a donation to help carry on the work).

Computer Feeds to Candidates.   Communication to supporters through the mails has raised money and educated Republican voters to the party's positions on issues, but a more intensive program of weekly computer feeds to candidates and party leaders has gone even further in developing a party line on issues. As it gets closer to the election, the frequency of the communication increases to up to five times a week. Each feed covers one issue and presents a speech outline, a possible press release, and is designed to help Republican candidates handle critical questions about the day's events and the administration's role in them. Those candidates who are elected to office will come to Washington with a common history on positions on a wide range of issues—positions written by professional party staffers. The program began in 1982 and has been refined and increased in subsequent elections. When the GOP loses the White House, it may lead to a far more homogeneous policy position and a far more critical role of the party in defining it.

Research. Although it used to be the case that campaign research was an activity designed to occupy volunteers more than to generate important information for the campaign, the field has grown far more important in recent years with the application of market research techniques and the capacity to synthesize and communicate vast amounts of information.

One critical departure made possible by the increased funds has been the greater application of tracking (retesting of poll respondents on a frequent basis). A classic example pointed to by Republican professionals was the 1982 Senate race in Missouri. John Danforth, the Republican incumbent, planned to run a positive campaign on his record. His opponent, state Senator Harriet Woods, (who herself came out of a media background) ran a surprisingly effective negative campaign against him, pointing to his being one of the richest men in the Senate. In the last few weeks of the election, the polls showed them about even. She ran out of money, however, and had to draw her ads for a week, but what the Republicans felt was the critical factor was their decision to run a more negative campaign against her—and their certainty they were right because of the tracking that showed the new campaign to be working. Danforth won re-election with one of the closest margins of victory in the country that year: 51 to 49 percent.

Data gathering has become an important role for the national party committees. The RNC monitors all newspapers, magazines, and broadcast networks, providing synopses to candidates and party leaders. The House campaign committee has the most comprehensive record of C-Span tapes (video recording of Congressional business) since the House began broadcasting. The House itself keeps tapes for only sixty days and the Library of Congress keeps audio tapes, but with the tacit agreement of both parties that the tapes will not be used. With the recent application of computer technology, the national party has also begun to maintain substantial records on opposition candidates: their votes, their speeches, any public utterance by them or about them. Its data base and retrieval systems are probably the most comprehensive in the country for a political organization.

What used to be known as "targets of opportunity," that is, examples of opponents engaging in what might be considered negative activities (voting the wrong way, and so on), have become far more sophisticated. The party can now provide information that Senator X failed to show up at a committee hearing, which consequently failed to get a quorum, which consequently failed to send out important legislation—and it was all the senator's fault.

One of the more effective advertising ploys in recent years are videotapes of opponents "shooting themselves in the foot." In 1984, Democratic Senator Carl Levin from Michigan was able to run an ad showing his opponent speaking to employees of the Toyota Company in Japan, telling them that he had a Toyota at home. The Levin campaign did not get the tape directly from the party, but it stands to reason that the permanent party organization is better able to retain and catalogue such moments than any other participant in the electoral process.

Most research expenditures are exempt from limitations imposed by the federal campaign finance law. The exception is survey research, which can be sold after fifteen days to a campaign at 50 percent of cost, and after sixty days at 5 percent of cost. Some things can be told about a campaign immediately if it is somewhat veiled: Your share of support is more than a third, but less than a half; your stand on position "X" is rated favorably by about half the voters; and so on.

Since both the House and Senate Republican Campaign Committees have now reached the stage where they can fund all of their candidates to the maximum allowed under the law—and they continue to raise additional money—the "excess" will increasingly be put into "soft" money programs such as research and genre advertising. According to staff sources, in the 1983–84 cycle, the Senate Committee raised $90 million, spent $25 million, paid off a $3.5 million debt, and after covering overhead expenses, put $6 million aside for the next election period. That sort of planning is just about unheard of in American party politics.

Television.   Although the Democrats now have the most sophisticated television capacity in Washington, the GOP has been exploring and expanding the use of video taping, cable, and other television vehicles to reach its own leadership around the country. Training candidates, explaining new programs, bringing selected persons into closed circuit communication with party leaders, and providing video opportunities for elected officials so that they can communicate with the voters at home are the most typical applications. The satellite facilities available to the Republicans enable them to "get the message" home almost immediately.

The power of the television medium assures it a continuing and growing role in American political life, matched only by the computer. There are, for instance, currently ten cable networks that accept local advertising, and it matters to political advertisers who watches USFL football and who watches tennis. A message about crime would be couched differently to the golf and tennis set, to those watching CPN and religious network programming, and to those who watch USFL and the Nashville network. The issue would be the same—the language and the appeal would be different.

Targeting audiences is hardly new; it has been the basis of all television advertising for many years. Political advertising has benefited from the experience and sophisticated market research of general advertisers who know, for instance, that the fans of "As the World Turns" on one channel may watch the local news on another channel. The message can be the same; it is just the rates that change.

Another wrinkle in the field of political advertising has been the development of a methodology which enables political spots to be pretested in a day or two, instead of the commercial market research method which can take as much as thirty days. Along with tracking, focus groups have been increasingly used by both sides (groups of eight or nine "real" people brought together to view an ad or discuss the campaign in depth). That capacity to learn more in depth about reactions—reaching the point where pollsters used rheostats to sample reactions during the 1984 presidential debates —along with the refinements in market segmentation have increased the use of television and, incidentally, been a major factor in the increase of campaign costs.

The Mondale/Ferraro campaign, in order to cut some of those costs, did away with testing in the latter phase of the campaign, relying instead on their intensive polling to tell them what message would be successful—for example, the Star Wars issue which came out of the debates. In the days preceding the second debate on foreign policy, the Mondale campaign ran a series of ads focusing on the message of Reagan's weaknesses they expected to get across during the debate. Republican tracking showed them that the message was having a negative effect and was, in fact, costing Mondale support among people who did not want to see Reagan attacked.

The Reagan/Bush campaign, on the other hand, did extensive testing on an ad showing a bear wandering through the woods. The ad was beautifully photographed and very sophisticated. The test showed that only a third of those who saw it understood it was a Republican political ad before the tag line at the end identifying it as paid for by the Reagan/Bush campaign, and then only another 20 percent understood it. In its favor, aside from pleasure the professionals took in its sophistication, it tested highest in recall and guaranteed it would be talked about for days after it was seen. It was so memorable, in fact, that Garry Trudeau did a take-off on the ad in Doonesbury three weeks after the election.

Technical Services.   The business of politics in the 1980s bears very little resemblance to itself in the decades before. The technological changes have been matched by the changes in law and in the expectations of the American electorate about how politics ought to be run. Federal, and often state requirements place a tremendous emphasis on accounting. The party can and does ease the burden of campaigns by providing advice, computer programs, and computer access to handle the work. During the 1980 election, the party computer staff wrote about 700 programs, processed more than 130 surveys for candidates, plus 5 national surveys, and handled more than 20 million names and addresses for voter registration and get-out-the-vote activities. It also surveyed data from 175,000 precincts in the country, combining the analysis with other relevant electoral data for the benefit of Republican candidates.[22] The services provided in 1984 were even more extensive, particularly at the county level where the national party was focusing much of its party rebuilding efforts.

The Case for Resurgence

During the 1970s, three things changed in American politics: the technology; the passage of complex federal campaign finance law; and the emergence of political action committees which institutionalized interests in American politics and, to some extent, fostered the growth of significance of ideology. We will describe the impact of the law in the appendix, and the interest groups on the parties in the following chapter, concluding this chapter with an analysis of what the activities and processes we have described add up to for the party system.

THE ACTIVISTS

The active membership of both parties has changed in the past two decades. There is a new generation of actors, tuned to the values and expectation's of today's political society. There will always be a need for generational change in the parties, and in politics, if the system is to remain healthy, but the characteristic that most distinguishes this generation from its predecessors is its interest in organization. Individuals within it have been touched from time to time with the passions of the years past and committed themselves to charismatic candidates and controversial issues, but they have been tempered by the disappointments of our time, and today, they tend to be more distant, more task-oriented, more professional. How much they represent the voters within their parties remains to be seen—in all probability they are (as always) more conservative or more liberal than their respective Republican and Democratic constituents—but their ideology is usually subordinate to their desire to win.

Both party staffs are better educated and more professional than those who used to fill party positions. The Republican staffs at both the national and the state levels are much larger than their Democratic counterparts, but the most important difference is not the quantitative but the qualitative difference between who is there now and who was there before.

One reason the Democratic staff appears much smaller is because it contracts out much of the work the Republicans do in-house, such as its direct mail campaigning. It is not a surprising difference given the traditional reliance Democrats have put on campaigns compared to Republican reliance on their party for campaign support. Nonetheless, the field of campaign consulting, which has grown dramatically in recent years, is just another reflection of the need of politicians to run for office with professional help. A good number of the consultants received their training in the party and then moved on to set up their own firms, helped along by party contacts and, in many cases, party urging that the candidate hire a consultant to oversee the campaign. Recently, however, the party has begun helping candidates avoid overcharging by consultants, by providing information about rates and so on.

Professionalization usually means that standards of behavior have been inculcated in the practitioner, that he or she is judged by peers, and that there is some formal process of accreditation to which the practitioner must submit himself. For our purposes, the professionalization of politics means that campaigns will become more homogenized, perhaps more nationalized. They will employ the same techniques, they will focus on those aspects of technical development which will advance the field: for example, new approaches to selling the candidate. Political scientist Larry Sabato cited former presidential candidate Milton Schapp's comment that he was "not trying to buy the election; I'm trying to sell myself!"[23] The selling will become more sophisticated, which may not be a bad thing. In itself that does not mean the candidates sold will be better or worse, but we would argue that the more candidates are selected by the professionals, the more likely they are to be worth selling because another standard by which the professionals will judge each other is the quality of the candidate and whether or not they win. This is particularly true of the professionals within the parties, as opposed to the private consultants, because they have a longer-range perspective and a closer body of supervisors.

The professionalization of the parties, and of politics in general, is a cause and effect of a different system of rewards. What distinguishes the professionals from their forebearers in party politics is a different set of rules of behavior, a different expectation of the spoils of victory. What distinguishes the professionals from the nonprofessionals is an understanding of the modern technology of campaigning and the intricacies of the law which effect the way money is raised and the distribution of campaign resources. What has not changed is the fact that each election is a choice that the voters must make based on the information the campaigns provide. Who provides the information (whether amateur or professional) is not as critical as the substance of what is said.

There is something of a cultural gulf existing between the professionals in both parties and many of the volunteers at the local level. One party worker described it as drawn between the wool vested and the polyester crowd. The fact that young people come out from Washington carrying the certainty that they know the answers, along with the fact that those they have come to counsel have often participated in politics for many years, adds up to resistance about turf, more than about questions of winning. It is the conflict of class and generation. It is the kind of conflict that has characterized the change in all organizations as they move from one era to another.

THE RESOURCES

In the two years preceding the 1984 election, the Republican party raised $225.4 million, almost four times the $57.3 raised by the Democrats in the same time period. The balance was an improvement for the Democrats who had been out-financed by five or six times in previous elections.[24] The Republicans continued to raise more money from individuals (five and a half times the Democratic proportion of individual contributions), but the Democrats raised four times the proportion of PAC funds, which are still a small, albeit growing proportion of party funding.[25]

The amount of money is phenomenal in its own right, especially if one considers that national party funds used to come entirely from the states in the form of assessments on the state committees. The amount of money is probably phenomenal for many reasons, but at the very least it is a measure of the financial strength of both parties at the national level. Money is not all that matters, even with that of-quoted comment of California politician Jess Unruh that "Money is the mother's milk of politics." It is an indication of well-being, and it is a first step toward the resurgence of party organizations.

The fact that the Republicans have raised so much money has

been widely noted for several years. For many political observers, the big question was whether or not the Democrats could ever catch up. David Adamany, President of Wayne State University, for instance, has argued that the base of the Democratic party will never yield the same financial results the Republican base has. According to Adamany:

> Contributing to politics is disproportionately an activity of the well educated, higher-income groups and of those who engage in other political activities as well. These groups are primarily Republican. . . . A further complication for the Democrats is the ideological division within the party. Givers . . . [are] much more liberal than the Democratic electorate. Since mass-mail appeals appear to be most successful when pitched to ideological groups, the Democrats may find responses to their mass-mail fund raising largely limited to the party's liberal wing, the smallest ideological group in population. . . . The Democrats draw the support of a vast majority of the nation's liberal activists, but the party is so diverse that it includes important groups of moderates and conservatives as well. It would therefore risk alienating important constituencies if it pitched its financial appeals to one ideological group within the party coalition.[26]

Only time will tell, but it should be noted that both parties have traditionally directed their fund raising to their more ideological wings: Republicans appealing to the more conservative; Democrats relying on the liberals. Even if liberals are the smallest ideological segment of the population, they are still large enough to fund a national party. As it happens, however, the party began expanding its contribution base to the rest of the Democratic constituency in 1981, reaching out to older voters on social security and prospecting many younger voters on a variety of nonideological issues with the sophisticated technology now available. The Democrats expect to catch up by 1988; certainly the potential base is there in the population among party identifiers.

The balance of party fund raising in the 1984 election does not make our case, but it does suggest the possibility that the Democrats will catch up. The rate of financial growth within the Democratic party is tied to three factors: the kind of fund raising it relies upon; the politics of the day; and the balance of power between the parties in the elective branches of government.

The Democrats began a serious shift to direct mail fund raising only after the 1980 election. The GOP began more than a decade before that, but began to see returns only several elections later. The large donors on whom the Democrats have relied since the Kennedy administration have been seriously circumscribed by the laws, and to some extent, by the loss of powerful incumbents in the White House and Senate. The shift to small donors is probably a necessity but a process which takes time and is not dependent on holding office. The argument could be made that the party out of power does better at direct mail solicitation because it has a more identifiable need to raise money. The fact that the GOP continued to out raise the Democrats once it regained the presidency is probably due more to the greater strength and sophistication of its list than to the fact of incumbency. It will take several elections for the Democrats to refine their lists and to train their donors to give to the party instead of the campaigns. Much of the perceived imbalance, after all, is due to the Democratic tendency to give to candidates rather than to the party which does make the elections, if not the party organizations, at least, more equitable.

HISTORICAL INEVITABILITY

Cornelius Cotter and John Bibby wrote an interesting article several years ago entitled "Institutional Development of Parties and the Thesis of Party Decline."[27] Their thesis was that American political parties tend to counterorganize. A thesis originally developed by V. O. Key, but applied in this instance to the national parties and their organizational structure. The theory is that if one party in a state is strong, the other will be strong; if one party dominates, it will be broken into factions, with the minor party behaving as another faction. One of the best examples of a strong party state is Indiana, in which both parties operate with a high degree of sophistication and skill, due in large part to the 2 percent kickback to the party permitted by those receiving patronage. On the lower end of the scale, the dominance of the Democratic party in the South has usually been described as a system of factions, in which the Republican party (until recently) participates as another faction. The new organizational strength of the GOP in the South has forced Democratic state parties to make changes, to offer more to their candidates, and to try to emulate in many instances what the opponents are doing.

At the national level, Cotter and Bibby point to the history of the development of national party committees and to the support structure behind them. Typically, it is the Republicans who take the lead in organizational development, with a lag of eight to twelve years (depending on when the Democrats lose the White House) before the Democrats catch up. If these political scientists are correct, the current imbalance between the Republicans and Democrats is characteristic of the lag time.

Perhaps the most important element in party balance is the nature of a two-party system. Whether the organizations are strong or weak, sophisticated or primitive, if the party out of power has a chance of replacing the party in power, it will never fall too far behind. It is the balance of power that assures equity in the equation, not the balance of structure, or even the balance of assets.

But the assets have grown, and the structure has changed accordingly. In the long run, the resurgence of the parties depends on their ability to capture the functions parties ideally possess: control of nominations; control of party resources in elections; influencing public policy; and as a vehicle for drawing individuals into the political culture.

The resources the national party can amass and distribute today cannot be matched by any other actor in the political process because of the restrictions the campaign finance law imposes, if for no other reason. It would be difficult for anyone to run for statewide or federal office as a Republican today without the support of their party. It would be surprising if the same thing would not be equally true of Democrats in a few year's time. Even today, Democratic candidates for federal office are more apt to first make a trip to Washington to see party leaders about the support they can expect from the party directly and from the network of PACs the party is capable of sending their way. In the old days, the first contact might have been more likely to go to the local party chairperson if not a private campaign consultant.

Party strength may come and go in American politics, just as the generations of political activists change and reflect the needs and values of their time, but the parties have demonstrated an endurance that challenges any institution in American history. The key to their success is their linkage to power. It may be that as power shifts the parties shift, that as interest in public power waxes and wanes, parties wax and wane.

It is unlikely the parties will disappear: too much is structured around them legally and culturally. Legislatures are organized by party representation. Voters may not see their political preferences as part of their sense of identity, but they do see political actors in terms of their parties and will vote on their estimation of how those politicians/parties behave. Morton Kondracke, a political journalist has argued that the decline in partisan identification has encouraged the parties to work harder; like the brokerage house, they are now forced to win the old-fashioned way: "They have to earn it."

> This has made elections more competitive across the country, which has made candidates more dependent on their party organizations.
> No longer can a politician in the South, for example, assume victory because he is a Democrat.
> He now has to run a more sophisticated campaign, and for assistance he must turn to the party organization, rather than, as before, simply taking advantage of the party name.
> On all levels, party aid to candidates—financial and strategic—has been growing incredibly.[28]

The changes in both parties in the past two decades have been enormous. The structures, the active participants, and the world around them have been altered. The increased financial resources at the national level in both parties (and the reversal of the flow of those resources from national to state instead of the other way around) have made many things possible. It may not be sufficient in itself to change the status of the parties in the public mind—it may not be necessary to change the status—but it is the necessary first step.

4

The Grassroots No Longer Count But the State Party Lives On

NOT TOO LONG AGO, in Indiana, a precinct captain knocked on the door of a house in his precinct and reminded the woman who opened the door that it was election day and she and the five other members of her family who were registered should make sure they got to the polls. A little later in the day, the party worker called and asked again when the family planned to vote. Before the polls closed, he called once more. They never made it.

About a year later, the woman came to see the precinct captain and asked him to help them get a traffic light put in at the corner. Life being what it is, the party representative looked her in the eye and told her that no votes meant no light.

Now that is a local party organization! At least, it was. There were other activities and other relationships that sustained our grassroots parties, but all of them were based on a quid pro quo, on incentives and rewards. The image of the local party we carry around in our collective recall of "The Old Days" is more upbeat than the nitty-gritty life of what it is precinct captains actually do. We think of rallies and picnics, tourchlight parades, and canvassers going door-to-door meeting their neighbors, telling them about the issues and the party's candidates. Whether or not every city and town ever reached that level of participation, the image is part of our political heritage and filters our expectations about what parties ought to be, if they are to be strong. Perhaps we should say, if they are to be "good" and strong, because the image carries within it the positive virtues we associate with parties.

Political campaigns were part of our entertainment and we gave them a good portion of our leisure time. Recently, our leisure time has grown but the sort of political participation we associate with the "good old days" has declined. It may not be a permanent situation, but it is likely to be characteristic of the remaining years of this century.

Changes have crept in to affect the nature of political participation: community ties have declined, and with less knowledge of our neighbors, we have grown more afraid of them, or at least less willing to seek them out or let them into our lives. We may live in greater physical isolation, but we are far more bound into the national culture by the communications media and advancement in high technology. We have different expectations of our lives in terms of family relationships, work, and health. All of these changes in us, and in our institutions and our attitudes about them, affect political identification and participation.

In this chapter we will explain why the grassroots have withered on the party vine, and why the decline of local parties is not synonymous with the decline of the party system. We will explore the role of state and local parties and their relationships to the rest of the political environment. We will conclude with consideration of the consequences of the nationalization of the parties and the effect a centralization of the political structure is likely to have on our concepts of democracy.

Changes in the Political World Which Affect the State and Local Parties

As at the national level, the most important recent structural changes in the state and local levels have been the growth of interest group participation through political action committees (PACs) and the changes brought about by campaign finance laws enacted by the states as well as the federal government. The changes have strengthened the state parties, and although they were not intended to weaken the local parties, they have added to the imbalance in resources available to the state and local parties.

POLITICAL ACTION COMMITTEES

It should come as no surprise that PACs, most of which were initially formed in response to the federal legislation, have become organizations in their own right within their parent organizations, and have expanded their scope of operation from federal candidates to state and local candidates. Business, particularly, lost ground influencing the outcome of the presidential selection process because of the greater value of volunteer-based organizations and the public financing provisions, and has concentrated resources instead at the congressional level and, increasingly, at the state level. Some states have moved to various forms of public financing to limit the influence of interests; sometimes candidates make their opposition to PACs part of their campaign strategy (especially if the other side appears capable of raising a great deal of money from them), calling for pledges to refuse PAC money, or making charges of "PAC Man" against their opponents. But these efforts notwithstanding, it is clear that PACs are active and are having an impact.

Political action committees are not necessarily autonomous organizations. Many are linked to networks with PACs representing similar interests, or as affiliates of national PACs or national organizations. The power of PAC involvement is not just the $5,000 it can contribute to a campaign (the amount may vary depending on state law), it is the number of PACs it can bring along with it to make similar contributions. The rush of PAC spending can and has begun to alter the balance between individual and interest contributions to campaigns, as well as the balance between in-state and out-of-state contributions. As one state party chairperson noted in 1978—an early year in PAC development—"Sixty percent of the money in the state is from outside—on both sides."[1] The data are difficult to assemble, but there is every indication that the trend toward out-of-state PAC money has increased a great deal since then.

According to Ruth Jones, a political scientist at Arizona State University who has studied state campaign finance for several years, there is a substantial increase in the amount of PAC spending in the states, particularly at the state (as opposed to the local) level.[2] It has led to a closer relationship between PACs and parties, enabling each to allocate resources more efficiently: PACs are introduced to candidates they might find appealing, and parties are able to divert their funds to more general campaign work. Freed of some kinds of candidate support, the state party can develop information, programs, and activities to be shared among several candidates. It can devote itself to recruiting candidates at the lower legislative level rather than paying attention only to state level politics. It can target limited resources to those elections it stands a greater chance of winning, and because there is less visibility at the lower levels, the smaller support it gives carries greater weight. Party leaders in the state legislatures are also in a powerful position to gather PAC support and allocate it to the re-election of their members and challengers.

Relationships between PACs and parties tend to increase PAC partisanship and there is some evidence to support that argument. Professor Jones cites the case of the principal business PAC in the state of Washington, for instance, which gave "34 percent of its money to Democrats in 1974, 26 percent in 1976, 22 percent in 1978 and only 5 percent in 1980." At the same time, the state employees' PAC contributions to Democrats went from 83 percent in 1974 to 92 percent in 1976 to 99 percent in 1980.[3] Although labor PAC money has always been highly partisan, business money has been more even-handed in distribution, if for no other reason than it needed to work with incumbent office holders, most of whom were Democrats.

FEDERAL AND STATE CAMPAIGN FINANCE LAW

Unlike the federal law, which places relatively severe restrictions on interest group giving to candidates and parties, only twenty-one states limit PAC contributions. Although it should be emphasized that the variation among the states is great and generalizations about them are offered with some license, it is legally permissible for many state parties to accept corporate funds, whether coming from a PAC or coming directly from the corporation treasury.

It is the legality of corporate giving at the state level that has prompted federal legislation to require separate accounts for state and federal elections, to assure that the federal candidates are running on "clean" money. Transfers of funds between accounts are permitted, but any transfer over $1,000 must be reported to the Federal Election Commission. The law also requires that the funds a party spends on its candidates be reflected in a proportionate allocation of overhead expenses: if the party spends $100,000 on federal candidates and $200,000 on state and local candidates, it must distribute the overhead on a one-third/two-thirds formula between its federal and state accounts. (See appendix for a more lengthy description of the federal campaign finance law.)

The law is complex and cumbersome and leaves a lot of room for confusion. If a congressional candidate stops by a pancake breakfast organized largely for state legislative candidates, the party must decide how much of the income and expenses are to be allocated to each account, which can be difficult if, for example, the federal candidate spent half an hour and the state candidates devoted the entire morning. In the early years of the federal law, most state parties participated in federal elections with trepidation (and no small measure of annoyance), while county and local parties were encouraged to get out of the business of supporting their congressional candidates entirely.

Those of us who studied the impact of the law in the late 1970s concluded that the federal campaign finance laws were hurting the parties, especially at the state and local levels. The concern was addressed in the 1979 amendments to the Federal Election Campaign Act (FECA), which among other things, lifted reporting requirements for expenditures for the use of property, the sale of food and beverages, and travel up to $1,000 per election in each category ($2,000 per calendar year) at the local level. While the amendments eased party spending somewhat in relation to the presidential election, the law maintained restraints on the parties vis-a-vis congressional elections. It assumes, for instance, that the state and local party are one committee and, therefore, limited in the total amount it can contribute ($5,000) to a congressional candidate, while permitting a higher limit of $17,500 for the national committee, which can/must also be shared between the national party committee and its Senate campaign committee for a Senate campaign. The House excluded its own elections from the joint contribution requirement in the law, thereby permitting an even higher national party contribution vis-a-vis the state and local party.

The campaign reform spirit that brought the Federal Election Campaign Act into being also brought changes in the states. Seventeen states provide public financing, in one form or another, for some of its candidates, although there are a number of variations in how the money is raised and how it is allocated, including what goes to the parties: some are excluded; some are conduits to candidates; and some parties receive funds with few or no restrictions.[4]

Although there is still debate about the consequences of all of this campaign reform on the state and local parties, there is little question that some of the regulations have strengthened the parties and some of the regulations have made party participation in elections more complex and, therefore, more problematic. The changes in the laws regarding parties are only a piece of the story explaining the role of parties in electoral politics: the dramatically increased role of PACs (admittedly from a base of almost zero in 1980); the limitations on individual contributions; the general rise in the costs of campaigning due to inflation in general (and higher costs in campaign expenses such as the media); and the increased professionalism required to run a successful campaign at any level of government all affected the position of the party and its committees. As with the law, some of these changes have strengthened the parties and some have weakened them.

The Role of State and Local Parties

If the national parties are primarily interested in national politics, it should be apparent that state parties tend to be interested primarily in state elections and, theoretically, local parties in local elections. Elections being what they are, however, everyone has an interest in the voter, and the problem the parties face is who—or which level of party—can best reach the voter. Tradition gives that function to the local party, but the increased reliance of campaign organizations on paid telephone canvassers, direct mail appeals, and the media reflects the recognition by the professionals that the local party no longer performs that function or, at least, no longer does it well.

STATE PARTIES

State parties are more like small versions of the national parties than they are like the local parties beneath them on the organizational ladder. They usually have a professional staff of one or two people in the Democratic party and several more in the Republican party. The resources which are supplied by the national party, and have included funds to hire staff, are an important factor on staff size and activity. Like the national structure, there is a state party committee and a chairperson and cochairperson (invariably a male/female balance). Typically, the committee is chosen by election, state convention, or caucus at the lower levels.

The state committee sends delegates to the national party committee, and, depending on the state, either plays a role in the selection of statewide candidates or makes decisions about the allocation of party resources among candidates. It may also determine party rules, although those are frequently controlled by state law and the national party. In most states, the influence of the state committee in determining who its nominees will be is severely curtailed by primaries, and the committees frequently do not attract the strongest leaders. Hotly contested presidential elections, or elections with unusually charismatic figures, often bring activists onto the committees because they want to influence the selection of delegates to the national convention. The campaigns of John and Robert Kennedy, Barry Goldwater, George McGovern, and Ronald Reagan seem to have left a heritage in the parties, as the "young Turks" of those campaigns have turned into the party regulars of the next election. The infusion of new blood with the presidential election has been one of the most important factors in the capacity of the parties to endure.

The interest associated with the presidential election notwithstanding, who wins the governorship or control of the state legislature are usually far more important issues to the state party than who carries the state in a presidential election. As for Congress, it has not been unknown for a state party to "kick someone upstairs" to the House or Senate as a way of getting them out of town (which some attribute, for instance, as the reason for New York's Alfonse D'Amato's rise to the Senate). Patronage in its many forms, from the award of a low-number license plate, to the placement of a traffic light, to a building contract, is far more characteristic of state politics than it is of national politics. The lower one goes in the political structure, the more concrete the rewards are apt to be, the more interest they generate, and alas, the more likely the political participants are to be susceptible to corruption.

THE RELATIONSHIP BETWEEN THE STATE AND NATIONAL PARTY

Presidential politics, although important to the state party because of the role the campaign plays in bringing people into politics in general and the party in particular, is typically addressed with tremendous hostility on both sides: the presidential campaign staff believes the state party is indifferent, incompetent, and often corrupt. Their perspective can be seen in a comment made by a presidential campaign worker: "You put in a quarter and you get back a dime."[5] According to another participant at the national level in 1980, "The only time the state party chairman is effective —matters—is at the presidential campaign. They have no fund raising juice on their own. They're not going to help a senator or a congressional candidate. Their only leverage is to be on the right side in the presidential contest."[6] Of course, what he means is that the presidential campaign is the only time the state party matters to him. He, and many of his national political colleagues, are completely oblivious to any other function the state party might have.

To the state party people, the presidential campaign is insensitive, indifferent to their concerns, and power hungry.

In the 1984 campaign, special efforts were made to alleviate the tensions, particularly by the Republican party which, among other things, hired a "mediator" to coordinate campaign/party activities through conference calls and daily meetings. Both parties are well aware of the problem and we will discuss some of the other solutions later in the chapter.

Emotions aside, there are real differences of interest at issue between the presidential campaign (which becomes almost synonymous with the national party committee every fourth year) and the state parties:

- Constituencies may not be identical: supporters of the presidential candidate may prefer the Senate or gubernatorial candidate of the other party, so resources spent in registration and getting-out-the-vote in one area may help the presidential candidate but hurt the rest of the slate.
- Presidential primary campaigns are often formed along factional lines within the state party so that one candidate's success means a victory for one faction and a loss of influence to the rest of the party. One effort to overcome that problem in recent years has been to place greater reliance on professional and volunteer primary campaign workers who travel from state to state during the primary season, trying to avoid relying on the locals. Jimmy Carter's "Peanut Brigade" of Georgia supporters in the 1976 campaign was one example which resolved the factional problem but opened the door to another problem of coming out of the national convention without the strong involvement of any leadership in the state party.
- Complicated and restrictive federal campaign finance law makes both sides wary of allowing the other too much leeway. This problem was more serious in the early years of the reforms because no one was sure what the law required, and both national parties actively discouraged the local parties, particularly, from participating in federal elections. The 1979 amendments which permitted limited local party spending eased some of the restraints, and the Republican party spent a great deal of money and energy trying to mount a grassroots program via the state and local parties, but the results thus far have yet to materially change the situation.

One important attempt to alleviate the tensions between the national and presidential campaign and the state party was the innovative, albeit somewhat controversial State Finance Program sponsored by the Republic party in 1980, with a smaller, but comparable program undertaken by the Democrats.

Federal law limits the amount of money an individual or a PAC can donate to federal candidates or the national party for federal elections (the aggregate limit is $25,000 to both). During the general election of the presidential campaign, no contributions are permitted to go to the candidates if they accept public financing. State law also often limits the money that can be contributed to the parties and its candidates. The loophole, or gap in the concepts of disclosure and limitations, is that the federal law is silent on what can be given to state parties, so it is possible for someone to give to many state parties, which would be reported (if at all) in the capitols of the states in question, but which would not be reported in the state in which the donor lived, or in Washington. The only knowledgeable parties would be the donor, the presidential campaign staff, and the national party which coordinated the transaction. It is just the sort of deal the campaign finance law was designed to reveal! As one state party chairperson noted, "We have lied to people and they have no idea of the money raised and spent."[7]

On the other hand, according to those who ran the State Finance Program in 1980, two-thirds of the money raised (which totaled approximately $9 million for the Republicans and $3 to $4 million for the Democrats who raised money less from individuals and more from labor unions and did not cross state lines in the process) went to state party overhead, with the rest going to get-out-the-vote efforts. The overall effect was to mitigate the inherent hostilities between the state party and the presidential campaign, and it was an organizational plus.

The relationship between the state party and the presidential campaign can also be exacerbated or relieved by the politics of the election at hand. In 1980, when Jimmy Carter was running for re-election, there was almost open warfare between the state parties and the national office because during the four years of the Carter presidency he considered the party to be no more than another special interest group. According to a former staff member of the Democratic National Committee:

> Carter, coming from Georgia, never saw the party as anything other than another interest group that had to be placated. He couldn't see that it would be to his advantage and there was a great distrust of the DNC, especially when Strauss was chairman, because he had been for Jackson. . . . [In 1980] they should have taken steps to have assured they would have the [party] money to spend, but they didn't build up the institution at all except to keep the Carter network alive. They froze the party out and harbored a grudge against state parties. . . . All state chairmen were the same—selfish and self-interested—unless they were with Carter early. They tended to express the view of Pat Cunningham: "The only thing the bosses are good for is to run against." When they hired their field staff, all they did was call their people, not the state party people.[8]

Incumbency is always a factor in intraparty relationships because the president will usually control, or seek to control, the national party committee. At the same time, a president such as Carter, who comes to office via the primary system and runs on a platform opposing the politicians, has little incentive to recognize the interests of state and local parties. His re-election campaign may try to cajole them; it may try to bribe them—it probably will not try to understand them. It is a problem faced by both parties.

The presidency notwithstanding, state parties have the capacity to amass resources and to benefit from the strengths of the national party. In that regard, they are like the national party. The only important organizational difference is the variable quality of leadership: good state party chairpersons may be more difficult to find year after year than good national party chairpersons. A poor leader could set any state party back, although it is not likely that the organization would tolerate much destruction, given its growing dependence on professional staffing which survives from year to year, and the incentive of every organization to maintain itself above all else.

LOCAL PARTIES

Throughout, we have focused on the great differences between the two major political parties at the national and state levels on the one hand, and the local levels on the other. The vast majority of local parties are essentially voluntary organizations. There are a few remaining local political machines (for example, the Nassau County Republican party in New York, and the Democratic party in Chicago), but they are rare. Most parties at the county, city, and town levels are made up of volunteers, with little organizational difference between Republicans and Democrats in those organizations.

Local parties are the weakest link in the party organizational chain. They have the least influence and the fewest resources. The combination of nonpartisan elections, primaries (where there are partisan elections), reliance on volunteers in an era when volunteers are hard to find, complex campaign finance regulations, and the general low regard in which parties are held combine to discourage the best leadership or the greatest participation.

As a nation we tend to think that some issues are, or should be, above partisan politics: education, crime in the streets, where the sewer or highway ought to run. In the early years of this century, the Progressive reforms succeeded in taking the parties out of these local issues by making the elections nonpartisan, but they remain potent political issues which often matter more to people than defense systems or tax programs and are apt to draw a bigger crowd to a meeting and galvanize local organization. Although we prefer partisan to nonpartisan politics, it is not our purpose here to argue the merits of that case, but only to point out that taking the party out of politics does not eliminate the politics and the compromises and trade-offs that go with it. It does redirect what might have been partisan energy into other organizations and, as such, is an added element in local party malaise.

Another factor in the weakness of local parties is the absence of a strong relationship between the various levels of the party. Although there is great variation between the states in how the parties are legally structured, in most instances, the lines connecting local to county and county to state are weak: level A has little authority and influence over level B, whether one expects the power to flow from the bottom up or from the top down. The weakness in the structural relationship, and in the organization as a whole, probably accounts for the fact that in most local and county level parties the number of positions available on any committee is likely to be greater than the number of persons who can be convinced to fill them.

The decline of the grassroots has been a major topic of concern for party activists and scholars, and almost every election in recent years has brought out new efforts to resuscitate local parties. We will describe two approaches which exemplify the problem and the probabilities of success in the long run. The first is the Democratic delegate selection process for the national nominating convention (undertaken really more to select a stronger presidential candidate than to rebuild local parties, but not unmindful of the latter objective). The second is a Republican party effort called the "Working Partners Program," which seeks to involve the party in local civic activity to recruit activists, rebuild the structure, and express the Republican commitment to the role of the private sector in solving social problems.

Delegate Selection.   The Democratic party reforms of the past several years call for the selection of delegates to the national nominating convention at the congressional district level and have generated a good reason for party members to get together and make decisions. In those states which hold caucuses to determine the distribution of delegates, the process draws considerable attention, but even those states which hold primaries must still hold meetings at the district level to decide who will serve on the delegation once the primary vote determines the proportion of delegates going to each candidate. Although the meetings are organized by the candidates more than they are by the parties, they are one of the few activities carried on under the party's aegis that has the capacity to bring people into politics, particularly national politics, at the local level.

There is an emerging belief that the caucuses are something of a mixed blessing as opportunities for citizens to exercise their civic responsibilities because the meetings can take an entire day (compared to the few minutes it takes to cast a vote) which can discourage people from participating, and the opponents can sometimes intimidate the faint of heart. On the other hand, these meetings can also bring a surprisingly vibrant element to modern presidential politics and certainly give a greater measure of control over the nomination to a larger portion of the most committed members of the party.

Working Partners Program. This program is one of several efforts undertaken by the GOP to rebuild the local party. It was first tried when George Romney was the governor of Michigan in 1960. Since then, it has grown to a national program which helps local parties undertake activities to benefit the community. The Colorado State party runs several refuges for the homeless in Denver; in New Mexico, the party helped assemble the resources to provide housing for senior citizens and raised $50,000 to build an indoor pool for handicapped children.

The Working Partners Program is an interesting departure for a political party because it raises questions about the role of a party and the likelihood of the success of this attempt to find a reason for existence at the local level. It may very well bring capable people into its ranks who will go on to run for office, or at least to participate more actively within their communities. It also has an ideological component compatible with the dominant mood of the GOP: government plays too great a role in social issues, responsibility for which should more properly be borne by the private sector. It is, therefore, the role of the local party to encourage its members to assume that responsibility and to set an example for the rest of the citizenry.

Refuges are a good example for our purpose because they bring to mind the role of soup kitchens for parties in an earlier era. In the days of the great political machines, the local party acted as a broker for those in trouble in return for their votes. This modern version of the helping hand, however, is not a recruitment mechanism directed at the recipients of the services as much as it is at those who provide it: the middle and upper middle-class Republicans who may increase their contributions to the party, will certainly be more inclined to vote Republican and, perhaps, to move from this activity to playing a role in electoral politics. This is not to say that an increase in funds is not a power in itself, nor that the sense of satisfaction for those who participate is not a worthwhile goal in itself. We want only to point out that this is an appeal to a different kind of incentive and offers a different reward than that employed by the machine bosses.

It may well be true that in those communities having benefited from such activities, the program has improved public perceptions about the Republican party (although it would seem to be an easy target for a Democratic retort that it is Republican policy in Washington that put the poor into the circumstances of needing private charity in the first place). But it is an activity subject to interpretation by both sides, and it is not apt to alter partisanship.

Whether or not there are public relations benefits, and whether or not the program succeeds in recruiting stronger candidates for office, the question remains of whether the activity is sufficient to sustain a local party—it is our judgement that it is not. What brings people together on a civic question may not sustain unity on political questions, particularly if the civic issue is local and the political issue is a national concern. Even the most ardent supporter of such good works should recognize that there are inherent differences between civic and political organizations. Belonging to an organization to provide a service and, usually, to benefit from the camaraderie that goes along with working with similarly-minded and similarly-situated persons in terms of social status is what motivates and sustains civic associations. Such groups are noted for their consensual nature.

Solidary benefits help political parties and even sustain them for periods of time, but they are not the primary reason for a party's existence. Such camaraderie, in fact, can be threatened by the heterogeneity a party requires if it sought to include both the givers and the receivers of services at such an intimate level over a long period of time (longer at least than a campaign season). Imagine the Junior League or Elks Club on the one hand, and the choices and styles of behavior of a political convention on the other.

Local parties can be sustained by commitments to issues (if the issues are large enough in scope to avoid significant divisions), by the search for power, and by the solidary benefits working together brings people. Their weakness is due to their lack of resources and their limited and episodic function. Political parties are about power. There is little power for local parties to contest because the majority of local elections are nonpartisan. The delegate selection process in the Democratic party could make a difference, but unfortunately, it happens only every fourth year. Civic activity is less likely to sustain a party because the solidary rewards are apt to be threatened by the conflict inherent in the search for power, and because they cannot be extended to the numbers of people a party needs without losing their appeal. We will consider other efforts to rebuild the grassroots later in the chapter, but we believe these two examples are clearly indicative of the problem.

Is Centralization Killing the Grassroots?

Nelson Polsby has made a strong argument against the notion of party centralization, asserting that the erosion of intermediary structures in general, and at the party level in particular, will weaken the legitimacy of the whole political system. He finds evidence for his thesis in the "palpable growth of disaffection with the Presidents and in the phenomenon frequently complained of— mostly by neoconservatives—and labeled 'ungovernability,' a pervasive inability of political leaders to satisfy the expectations of voters."[9] It was one of the purposes of the recent Democratic reforms to correct this problem of legitimacy and absence of faith, but instead, according to Polsby, the reforms have exacerbated the problem.

It is our view that we have all ignored the real causes of local party decline and erroneously placed the blame on the recent reforms, which, we now believe, may do more to help the cause of local parties than almost anything else in recent years. It was the Progressive reforms of nonpartisan elections and primaries that did the most damage to the local parties, but the past notwithstanding, it has been the change in organizational needs and motivation which really altered party structure: Chiefly responsible for these alterations are the decline of volunteers; the increased reliance on professionals who can apply the new technologies of communication and persuasion; the capacity to generate resources at the top; and so on.

The volunteers, who have disappeared for a variety of reasons from the local scene, have been replaced by professionals at the state and national levels. When the local party functioned at its best, it too, was run by professionals of a sort (at least by people motivated with a solid material reward in mind). Professionalism, while not synonymous with centralization, is part of the nationalization process. It means, among other things, that the people who participate in campaign battles expect to go on from one campaign to the next and take pride in their craft. They develop techniques and they study the practices of their opponents. They even come to recognize a shared set of interests with the opposition. They know the rules of the game and how far they can be bent.

Both national parties have been mindful of the decline of the grassroots. They believe that with new leadership and with increased levels of skill at the top they will be able to solve the problem. Although we think that there is more rhetoric and wishful thinking involved in the process, there is no question that both parties, but particularly the Republicans, have devoted considerable money, time, and energy to the issue.

TRYING TO REBUILD THE BOTTOM FROM THE TOP: THE REPUBLICAN EFFORT IN 1980

In the mid to late 1970s, after the GOP had accrued the resources and capability that define it today, its political energy was directed toward campaigns rather than either the state or the local party. It did not entirely ignore state parties, providing funds for one or two full-time staff positions and a regional coordinator (the regional staff has grown considerably in the past several years), but it did discourage the local parties from participating in federal campaigns. During the 1980 election, with the impetus of a presidential election, the RNC tried to address the problem of the grassroots directly now that there had been several years of experience under the campaign law. "Commitment 80" was, in its own words:

> a nationally coordinated and locally implemented program to turn out hundreds of thousands of people on a given day at the designated time to walk their neighborhoods and communities for the Republican Party and Ronald Reagan. Its objectives . . . include advocacy, voter identification and voter turnout.[10]

"Committment 80" was designed to perform the role of a local party during a presidential campaign. Its failure (attested to by party workers during interviews after the election) was attributed in part to the novelty of the approach: the national party did not have much experience mounting such an effort (having devoted itself more to campaigning and state party building in the past few years) and expected to learn from their mistakes; and in part to the belief that grassroots campaigning works only when you have the candidate actually in tow (an argument made by people at the state level as opposed to those in Washington).

In 1984, the Republican party effort fared better, partly because of the impetus given it by Jesse Jackson's threat to register black voters, and partly because it tried to learn from the 1980 experience. Efforts were focused at the county level, especially at those counties which could mount a professional staff of their own to sustain it. There was far more mixing of volunteers with professionals than occurred in 1980. Some of the grassroots tasks were entirely undertaken by paid workers. The party was probably both helped and hurt by the fact that it did not have to go through primary campaigns: it was less divisive (and special efforts were made in the campaign organization to bring together participants who had not been with Reagan in 1980); but it also had less of an opportunity to be tested. Although, in the view of the party staff, the results were mixed with not more than a handful of counties in each state making any substantial gains, there was far more enthusiasm for the county programs by the party field workers in 1984 than there had been for the grassroots program in 1980.

Would it have mattered to either of these efforts if they had come from the local level rather than the national office? Not if the assessment that the motivation for volunteers to go door-to-door has declined with the changes in our social attitudes and economic needs is correct.

Looked at from the perspective of incentives, if people used to go door-to-door because they believed they had to pay their dues to an organization that would find them a job, or see to it that a traffic light appeared on the corner, they would do so. If they no longer needed the party to get the job or mediate transactions between themselves and the powers downtown, those people, at least, would not knock on doors. They might come to a campaign headquarters staff to stuff envelopes because that is a more social activity than the lonely exercise of canvassing, and it would still satisfy that inchoate desire to perform some civic service. They might canvass if they believed strongly in the importance of the election out of a purposive or ideological consideration, and/or if they believed their participation would really make a difference.

Even though Ronald Reagan has turned out to be one of (if not *the*) most ideological presidents, the Republican party was hard-pressed to find an incentive that worked in 1980. Another candidate, another approach to the election, another election with different issues might have a different result, but we doubt it. Reagan's candidacy proved successful in the general election in spite of his ideology, not because of it. It was the unpopularity of incumbent Jimmy Carter in 1980 and the personal popularity of Reagan in 1984 that won the voters approval. Issue activists certainly abounded in religion and abortion, particularly, but it was the interest groups that organized them and got them out on the street, not the party.

There are three possible solutions to the problem of local party decline: giving a significant role to participants (by which we mean the party activists); motivating participation by appealing to purposive (that is, ideological, moral, or other issue) concerns; or eliminating the expectation of maintaining a local party from the American party system. The Democratic reforms, which have also affected the Republican party to some extent, were designed to address the first question; the nature of national communication from both parties may have solved the second problem. We will address the third alternative at the conclusion of this chapter.

PARTICIPATION AT THE INTERMEDIARY LEVELS

In 1976, when the party reform process was at its height, more than 70 percent of both parties' delegates were chosen in thirty primaries.[11] In 1980, there were thirty-three primaries and thirty in 1984. Throughout their history, primaries were designed to take the party out of the decision-making process, to extend the franchise of party nomination to the voters, without benefit of any intermediaries. Although the national parties would prefer to have fewer primaries—everyone pointing longingly to the 1960 election when John F. Kennedy won the Democratic nomination after being tested in four primary elections—it is a decision made in each state based on the value a primary election would have for the state party in particular and the state's economic well-being in general because a primary will attract many, if not all of the candidates and the national media (which can easily outspend the campaigns).

The recent increase in caucuses, and more importantly, the Democratic delegate selection rules that require a caucus process, even when there is a primary to select the individuals who will attend the convention, have gone a long way toward breathing new life into the local party, at least with regard to national politics. We believe this effort is an important step in party resurgence which links the local and national parties together nicely.

Even in today's world of declined volunteerism, coming to a meeting in the neighborhood would not be particularly onerous. It offers the sociability that has maintained parties in the past, and it does not interfere with private lifestyles. It is not dependent on a material reward, but rather relies on the purposive motivation of issues or candidate preference. Unfortunately, doing it only every fourth year is not sufficient to maintain a local organization.

USING ISSUES TO BUILD LOCAL PARTIES

Issues can attract, but they can also divide, which brings us to the question of whether a local party can be sustained on national or local issues, and beyond that, to the broader subject of ideology. Because ideology has never been a major factor in American political life, we are using the term rather loosely to denote general attitudes about government: Democrats leaning to the left, favoring the idea that government has a responsibility to play a mediating role in society; Republicans leaning to the right, opposing the notion of governmental interference in private life. Who is hawkish and who is dovish often depends on the question of who is in control of the White House and running the war. Both parties can sound remarkably alike on foreign policy issues, although rarely at the same time.

The national interests more or less align themselves with the national parties within the rubric of these attitudes about government (the disadvantaged tending to appeal to the Democrats and business interests leaning Republican), but the interests (as organized groups), and the issues (as topics requiring public action) are not always aligned: the groups may have an alliance with some members of Congress which crosses their traditional party preference; the debate on an issue may have extended the subject in such a way that a group's interest may be better served by the other party. The very complicated Simpson-Mazzoli bill on immigration which came and went several times in 1984 is a good example of groups perceiving themselves best served first on one side and then on the other. The coalition of groups changed as did the position of the Democratic party.

Decision making aside, issues have come to play a critical role in fund raising for the national parties and that fact has assured an increased centralization of issue positions for the party as a whole. There is not likely to be a turning back, given the rewards in resources and influence. The impact of issue centralization remains to be seen, however. Does it become replicated at the state and local levels by similar appeals to positions that strongly motivate voters? Does it require state and local parties to submerge their differences with the national organization in order to continue receiving benefits? And will it, in the long run, force both parties to more extreme positions, making it more difficult for voters to risk a change?

A strong criticism often voiced about local parties is that they abdicated their responsibility to take positions on issues and that the vacuousness of the organization is the reason for its decline. If local parties took positions on local issues, it is possible they would come to have meaning to voters, especially in the light of the decline of other incentives.

There is, however, a problem in taking a position on local issues: it can risk alienating a good portion of the party's constituency. A proposed highway running through a wildlife preserve or through a residential district might seriously divide a community along the lines of who lives where and who enjoys what sorts of leisure activities. There is a certain amount of political homogeneity within neighborhoods, making possible partisan appeals based on zip codes, but the conformity is not so high as to assure local interests would not divide residents within a party.

Are there local variations in national issues which a local party can identify? In some cases that would clearly be possible, and the Republican Working Partners Program undoubtedly has identified a number. In some cases, local issues are more idiosyncratic. The problem for the local party is that intensity is likely to be far greater on local issues than their national counterparts, and if they are not inherently partisan (in the national sense), they may be divisive at the local level. Condominium conversion versus rent control can be very divisive in urban areas and one's position usually depends on one's circumstances. Where to build a highway is not the same question as whether or not a public authority ought to build a highway.

It would appear that there is a wide scope for local acceptance of national positions, but it is not unlimited. If local parties are to use issues as a motivation for participation, they may be constrained to find issues that echo issue positions taken on by the national party, or at least issues which do not run counter to the national party. Looking at the record, the issues the national parties have adopted most successfully (in terms of consolidating support, influencing public policy, or raising funds) have fallen into three categories: the issue has already found significant support among party activists, such as the ERA for Democrats; the issue is current and does not have a standing constituency, such as the Panama Canal Treaty for Republicans; or the issue is of such a broad nature that it does not relate to any specific action, such as appeals to patriotism, bringing down the deficit, and so on. Local issues would, presumably, have to fall within the same bounds.

There are a host of other issues upon which the Republican party, particularly, has done research and taken positions. While they may not mobilize large segments of the population in every election district, they may carry more weight in some districts. As we noted in chapter 3, one of the important new services the national party provides its candidates on these issues is information, speech outlines, and so forth. And one of the benefits to the national party is having its successful candidates come to Washington already committed on a wide array of what might be called "peripheral" issues. This peripheral homogeneity is a product of centralization and works against local autonomy to some degree.

Is the American Party System Dependent on Decentralization?

Party power in America has traditionally been held at the state and local level, when power could be said to be held at all. The consequence of holding power locally was an idiosyncratic collection of local parties, which combined to assure a weak national system. The consequence of a strong national party would seem to be greater conformity in the local parties because of the uniformity of services provided, more cohesion on issue positions, and, perhaps, on the quality of candidates who would be recruited and trained by the party organization. Would this overlay of uniformity threaten the regional and cultural differences that exist and that have led to the differences among the state parties? If a strong, centralized system did threaten the diversity, would that matter in the long run?

As we noted in chapter 3, there are many reasons for the existence of different interests in the country: geography, ethnic origins, many centers of power, the separation of powers, and so on. Most of those causes of diversity remain, although the distances have been somewhat diminished in significance because of the increase in communication. It remains unlikely that the United States will ever become so homogenized that urban populations will share the same lifestyle and values of rural populations; that those living in the sun belt will have the same concerns as those in the snow belt.

If the diversity remains, and the national parties are staffed by professionals interested in winning elections, we believe there will be little threat to the sense of autonomy we cherish for the local systems. A threat exists only if ideologues take over the national parties and insist on issue purity.

PRESSURES FOR CONFORMITY

Pressure for ideological purity can be the most powerful incentive for uniformity, and the question must be asked if we are becoming more ideological as a nation, and if a strong central party system would not hasten the process. It is our contention that when a party moves too far from the center in a two-party system, it risks failure at the polls and may eventually be replaced if it does not shift back to a more moderate position. An interesting case of such moving about the ideological spectrum may be unfolding in Great Britain, which, although a parliamentary system, functions more or less like a two-party system.

For the past several years the Labour party's structure and ideology have moved it further to the left, causing some of its moderate leaders to leave and form the Social Democratic party (SDP). The SDP formed an alliance with the Liberal party (which for years was itself dominated by issue purists who are now beginning to think of themselves as becoming more professional with the prospect of governance seeming more realistic), and together they are trying to appeal to the middle left, hoping that the Alliance will eventually replace Labour as the second party alternative to the Conservatives. Labour's ability to move back to a more moderate position may have been somewhat curtailed by the loss of the moderate leaders and by the attempt of the Alliance to fill that void.

While both American parties have moved further apart, with some important realigning going on between them, especially in the South, it has not led to the creation of a potentially effective alternative. At least, not so far. Groups of the disaffected have split off from the Democratic party and attempted to create a third party, but they have invariably been groups further to the left such as the Citizens party formed in 1980. The Republican party may become a more critical case. It has been moving to the right since 1964, but appears to have accelerated the pace in the 1984 election. The election suggested that Ronald Reagan was sufficiently popular to win, but the positions of the party were not shared by a majority of the electorate, and his coattails did not go very far. If the party continues to move to the right and loses Reagan as its standard bearer (as it will in 1988), it risks losing office. It is at that point that the question of realignment will have be faced: if the majority of the population have accepted Reagan's solutions, the population will become more conservative (and there has already been movement in that direction); but it is also possible that many will not be so convinced and will re-evaluate their partisan choice when both parties offer new candidates. If the Republicans lose, and lose consistently, they will have to re-evaluate their place on the ideological spectrum.

Some would argue that the process has already begun because the party platform in 1984 was less conservative than the 1980 GOP platform, with the exception of the ERA and right-to-life planks, because the 1980 platform called for the abolition of the Departments of Education and Energy as well as the deficit and military superiority.

Our point in even making a prediction about party ideology is that there is a possibility that a centralized political system that becomes ideologically coherent can threaten the diversity we associate with a weak, decentralized party system. We believe the danger of that happening is checked by the essential need of the party to win election. If the parties are too far apart in their conceptions of how the world ought to function, the party out of power will not be able to function as an umbrella for the disaffected of the party in power. The out-party must appeal to the voters who elected the in-party; it must, therefore, offer a platform that is not radically different from its opponent's. It may not be correct to suggest that our centrist tradition and our two-party structure guarantee moderate politics, but they certainly encourage it.

A more subtle area of national party influence and the pressure for conformity has to do with the training of party workers: those who staff the state committees and regional offices, and those who run the campaigns. The professionalization going on in both parties encourages a similarity in approach and in preferences: certain kinds of candidates will be thought to be more winnable; certain techniques will be applied to almost all campaigns. It is not so much an overt pressure from the central office as much as it is the desire every candidate and campaign organization has to be up-to-date.

If everyone comes from the same school, they are apt to think alike. They are certainly apt to act alike, which will account for conformity in campaign techniques. Some of the old standby campaign activities will be discouraged as in a 1984 Oklahoma congressional campaign, in which one of the authors was the professional consultant. One of the campaign workers insisted that she organize a grassroots canvassing effort. Although the consultant counseled against it and directed the campaign's resources elsewhere, he did not forbid it, asking only that the campaign worker not rely too heavily upon it. The persuasion may be gentle, but the direction is clear: it is taught in the campaign schools run by both parties; it is counseled by the paid professionals. The effect is that grassroots canvassing efforts will fall by the wayside unless and until the professionals think they will make a difference.

The techniques are not the only connecting links; the people who employ them are beginning to get to know each other. After the 1980 election, there were several occasions that brought together members of the staffs of the two national parties. Below the level of party chairperson, few of them had ever met before. Their shared concerns included the impact of campaign reform and the rise of PACs. Those who organized the conferences (including the Institute of Politics at Harvard and the American Assembly at Columbia University) encouraged the party people to work together. For some it was a long journey. One White House staffer who came to his position after a lifetime in Washington and several years at the RNC, told one of the authors that until he met Larry O'Brien (just a few months before the conversation in 1981), he thought all Democrats had horns and was amazed to find the former DNC chairperson to be an intelligent human being with a keen sense of humor.

The professional association of political consultants, which was originally populated by academics and rather peripheral campaigners using it for the legitimacy it provided, has grown considerably with the increasing participation of the leading firms in the field on both sides. All of this activity adds up to a common approach in attitudes, behavior, and technique: to a centralization of political style as well as structure. Elections being as unpredictable as they are, it does not entirely exclude amateurs, but it does influence the behavior of political activists who look to each other for approval, and it is a change from the past.

Besides ideology and the seeming inevitable spread of conformity in technique and style, are there other threats to our sense of democracy in a centralized party system? One important party function is control over nominations. Certainly the efforts by the Republican party to recruit and train candidates threatens the concept of local party autonomy if one assumes local parties might promote other candidates, but the situation has been something altogether different in recent years. It is not so much that the national party is moving in on the local turf as much as it is that the national party is intruding into what has become a system of self-selected candidates.

If the national party plays a greater role in candidate selection and campaign support, it stands to reason the party will have greater influence over that candidate's performance in office ("greater" in this instance is clearly a relative term). Evidence of the increased role can be seen (aside form the efforts of the national committees of both parties) in the growth of the Democratic and Republican congressional and senatorial committees.

The Democratic Congressional Campaign Committee, under the leadership of Representative Anthony Coelho, raised $5.7 million in 1981–82, compared to $1.8 million raised by his predecessor in 1979–80. It was, of course, far below the comparable Republican committee, which raised $54.3 million, but it was the critical first step by the Democrats to emulate Republican success.[12] Under Coelho's leadership, the committee has redirected its resources away from incumbents, who had been the chief beneficiaries in years past, and begun targeting promising challengers. Coelho went after business PACs, not leaving that growing field to the GOP unchallenged, and under his tenure the new Democratic television facilities, which make it possible for office holders to communicate in a very effective way to their home constituencies, have forced the Republicans to redesign their efforts to keep up with the state of the art.

The increased strength of the campaign committees means that the national party has more to offer its nominees, and if it offers more than any other group, it will clearly be more influential with

those candidates. The state and local parties do not have comparable legislative committees to look after their candidates so the
sphere of national party influence in congressional elections, at
least, is as likely to remain unchallenged as it is to grow.

The stronger the party at the national level, the more emphasis
placed on professionalism, and the techniques associated with it,
the weaker the local party becomes, if only because it is seen in
relative terms. What is lost in the process is not the function that
the local party performed of communicating to voters, because that
role can be performed just as well if not better under a centralized
system through direct mail and professionally staffed telephone
banks. What may be lost is the opportunity local party participation provided to those who want to play a more active role. The
amateurs are less important. Of course the campaign schools in
their many forms have the capacity to turn many of those who
want to participate into professionals. Access to the technocracy
of politics remains, but it is more focused; it is, therefore, less open.

Professor Polsby's concern about the loss of the intermediary
structures had more to do with the sense of legitimacy than it did
with the accessibility. It is our sense that unless one assumes amateurs are inherently more legitimate than professionals, the question of legitimacy is really a concern of the voters and what they
believe to be a fair and proper process. The "best" parts of the
system, the ones we like to recall, are the local activities that
generated enthusiasm, commitment—legitimacy. Some of those
activities remain as part of every candidate's campaign, and it does
not really matter whether they are organized by amateurs or
professionals. Some of the activities are just no longer as popular
as they once were. Some activities have been lost and we should
mourn their passing, but we would conclude this discussion with
the rather controversial proposal that the grassroots no longer
functions in American politics as it once did, and despite the
memories it evokes in our civic sensibilities, its departure from the
scene may not be so catastrophic for the democracy as it seems
because it does not affect the flow of information to the voters and
does not give one candidate an unfair advantage over another.

All local parties are not alike. Some retain important functions,
particularly, and perhaps exclusively, when they have a role to play

in local elections. We would exclude these parties from the destiny
we foresee for those without such contests to sustain them. Besides
door-to-door canvassing, all of the other labor-intensive activities
of campaigns have been threatened: telephone canvassing is now
done more by paid professionals than volunteers; even that old
standby research (an activity campaigns used to undertake more to
satisfy the desires of volunteers who wanted to feel important than
to learn something relevant for the election) has become important
and has been taken over by the professionals. It should come as no
surprise that stuffing envelopes can be efficiently handled by machines, usually the machines under the direct control of the direct
mail companies miles removed from the campaign headquarters.
The need to communicate to voters remains, but the capacity to do
so through the mails, the telephone, and the media far exceeds the
ability of a local organization, whether party proper or campaign.
The only circumstance when it does not pay to go to the media or
to rely on the sophisticated professional outreach available to campaigns today is when the targeted area is small, that is, when the
election is local. Unless and until nonpartisan elections are replaced with partisan contests, the local parties will have no sustaining function and will eventually die away.

No one—least of all those who run for the chairmanship of the
national parties—wants to recognize or admit the long-term weakness of local parties as institutions. To do so sounds undemocratic.
So does urging a return to partisan elections. We believe that
democracy can stand the strain, and, given our optimism about the
future of the national and state parties, we strongly suspect that all
of those characteristics we aspire to in an informed electorate and
a responsible republic are available to us now: communication;
coherence in choices; and accountability. It is entirely possible that
if we let go of the memory, we might even develop alternatives to
the functions the local parties used to perform, especially the entry
it provided many citizens into public life.

PART

III

THE PARTY
AND POLITICS

5

Why the Interest Groups
Can't Beat the Parties

INTEREST GROUP ACTIVITY is probably the most controversial issue in politics in recent years. Sometimes the charge is
made that the interests, which have always been suspect, are now
all powerful in the electoral process with PAC contributions.
Sometimes the charge is made that the interests are behaving like
wild cards because of independent spending. Sometimes we fear
they will—or already have—taken over the parties. We are afraid
that some interests are too dogmatic, too ideological. Some interest
groups have come quickly upon the scene, and that, too, frightens
us, because we do not really know who they are and what they
intend to do in the long run. And, certainly, we are cautious about
the nature of some of the new issues: many are moralistic; almost
all are divisive, or at least represent significant divisions within the
society. Whether new or old, all of the campaign finance regula-

tions enacted in the 1970s—in fact, throughout our history—have been directed at curbing the interests, one way or another.

It is our contention that the interests will never dominate the parties. It may take an election or two, but the parties always have a moderating effect on the interests in time. Interests, by definition, never represent majorities in the population. That role of forming majorities is uniquely a partisan role and it can be accomplished only by seeking compromises among interests and consensus within the population. It is not an activity interests can undertake on their own because they have little with which to bargain; their leaders would be in jeopardy for their positions if they offered to give away too much.

WHO ARE THE INTERESTS?

Let us begin by considering who or what we are talking about. It verges on the simplistic to point out that there are always interests in politics, but some are more acceptable than others. Interests, for our purposes, are groups that have a desire to influence public policy. There may be a direct economic benefit they are seeking to achieve, such as a relief from taxes or a ban on imports; they may be devoted to a larger concern, such as saving the environment for future generations, or saving unborn fetuses from abortion. Although conflicting interests are integral to the functioning of a democracy, it is part of the American political ethos to decry them for their selfish behavior and to fear them for their unbounded power. Much of our public energy is devoted to curbing somebody's interest. More and more of us belong to more and more interests and sometimes we find them conflicting. Life, in that respect at least, is not getting any easier.

Interests may be corporations, associations of volunteers, associations of professionals or corporations (such as trade associations), a professional group representing nonprofessionals (such as unions), or just a group of professionals representing an issue. Most of the established interests have some form of accountability built into their organizational structures: they have elected or appointed board of directors that meet and make policy and/or hire professional staffs, they may have chapters or other kinds of divisions that provide for participation by members around the country. Some of the controversy surrounding the newer groups is that they are accountable to no one: they are small groups of professionals, based in Washington, with paper boards that rarely if ever meet. The activity undertaken by an interest may be undertaken by a single individual instead of a group, to benefit himself, a larger issue, or just to demonstrate that he has influence. An individual, clearly is only accountable to himself.

Some interests seem more acceptable than others. They may be credible because we agree with them, or because we have just grown accustomed to them. Historical accident accounts for some of the acceptability: groups formed in earlier eras (and managed to survive beyond the hot hostile days that brought them into being) are known entities and have generally worked out a role for themselves in the scheme of political life. Labor is allied with the Democratic party: it gives money to the party's candidates, it provides candidate organizations with volunteers, and it advertises support among its membership. The American Medical Association, through their political action committee, AMPAC (the second oldest political action committee in the country after labor's Committee on Political Education, COPE), endorses candidates, provides funds, takes out advertisements announcing its support in the general media. Doctors are notoriously poor donors themselves and rarely have the time to volunteer, but will lend their names to causes.

Interest groups tend to form in cycles and to counterorganize. Some eras lend themselves to public divisiveness more than others: the Progressive Era and World War I was followed by a curiously quiet political decade in the 1920s; which was followed in turn by the highly politicized 1930s and World War II. The 1950s were the quietest yet, followed by the very turbulent late 1960s and early 1970s. As issues become political, when debate widens and divisions coalesce, both sides of an argument form organizations and seek to have an impact on the decision makers and the public at large. The nature of the organization reflects the time and the values then current more than it does the division on the issue. Thus Americans for Democratic Action, a leading liberal organization formed in the late 1940s, is a membership organization with a centralized decision-making style, whether of its national professional staff in Washington, its national board, or the state boards around the country. Organizations with similar objectives, which grew out of the movements and experiences of the 1960s, tend to be less centralized, emphasizing the participation of their membership at the grassroots level. The differences in style can make it difficult for the organizations to build coalitions when the relationships and decisions must be worked out at something other than the staff level.

Most of the interest groups we accept as legitimate members of the political world can be said to be held in some form of accountability for their actions. They may be membership organizations like Common Cause or the National Rifle Association, or an umbrella group over many organizations such as the Chamber of Commerce and all of the trade associations. They may be made up of a relatively small set of participants such as the National Council on Foreign Relations, or they may represent a mass membership such as the American Automobile Association. Legitimacy can depend on who and/or how many citizens an interest can claim to represent and how credible their behavior has been in the past. The power an interest can expect to generate will depend on the resources (principally, but not entirely, money) it can raise and spend, and on the influence it has over its membership and the public at large. Unions used to be more powerful when the support of labor leadership was reflected more consistently than it is today in member voting.

There is an assumption that interests, which have been around for awhile and which have become part of the political landscape, have established their place in the scheme of things. They have friends; they have enemies. They usually have a variety of concerns in which they are interested, and the organization's survival is not tied to the success or failure of any given battle. The standard operating procedures they develop over time keep them within the bounds of propriety. Participating in illegal acts endangers their credibility (and possibly their survival) and the professional staffs that generally run these organizations are not apt to go too far.

WHAT WE FEAR ABOUT INTERESTS

Time, and the nature of the organization's structure and processes, and some measures of accountability are important factors
in their acceptability. But what is it that makes them, if not illegiti-
mate, at least worthy causes of concern?

Corruption: Direct and Indirect.   Clearly, how an interest seeks
to further its aims is one of the most important factors. If it gives
money surreptitiously, or provides other kinds of services or gifts
that are not visible and not openly reported, it will be suspect at
the very least. Much of the Watergate scandal was about the contributions the Committee to Re-Elect the President solicited from
corporate America and what those companies expected or actually
received in return for support of the Nixon campaign. The disclosure provision of the campaign finance law written following Watergate was one of the most effective pieces of legislation in campaign reform. While not entirely eliminating the possibility of
corrupting influence, it undoubtedly curtailed the behavior of some
and it has strengthened the confidence of many in the system.

Disclosure has added to the sense of legitimacy of interest group
participation in some respects, but its very visibility has convinced
others that the amount of money pouring into political campaigns
is corrupting, almost by definition. Elizabeth Drew in her book
Politics and Money: The New Road to Corruption argues that
"What matters is what the chasing of money does to the candidates
and to the victors' subsequent behavior. . . . The point is what
raising money, not simply spending it, does to the political process.
. . . What the whole thing is doing to the democratic process."[1]

How much money anyone raises or spends is always a relative
question, and although scholars have argued for more than a decade that we spend more money to advertise soap than we do to
communicate information about our candidates for public office,
there is no question that much more money is spent on campaigns
than used to be the case. Spending in the 1980 presidential campaign, for instance, increased by 56 percent over the 1976 race,
although if controlled for cost of living increases, the rate of growth
declines to 21 percent.[2] PAC spending is far greater in congression-

al races than presidential campaigns because of the value matching funds places on individual donations during the primary season and the prohibition against any giving during the general election when the national party nominees are supported, in theory at least, entirely by public funds. In a 1984 Senate race in New Hampshire both party candidates raised close to a half a million dollars each from political action committees, far more than was ever raised or spent in New Hampshire before.[3] Although New Hampshire is one of the smaller states, much of its media originates in Boston, which substantially increases campaign costs because of the size of the Massachusetts television market.

As it happened, in neighboring Massachusetts, the threat of appearing to be owned by the interests led to another phenomenon: pledges by candidates against taking PAC money. This mini-movement was also seen in the Democratic presidential primary race and in other races around the country in 1984, with accusations of "PAC Man" flung by one candidate against another. Whether it survives as a trend remains to be seen, but it is due to the visibility of interest group giving more than it is to the fact of interest giving. The argument against Elizabeth Drew's thesis has been made by many political observers, such as Michael Malbin, of the American Enterprise Institute. He has noted that "it takes a large set of blinders to miss the fact that the emergence of PACs represents an improvement over what went on before."[4]

In fact, very little is known of what went on before (which is part of Malbin's thesis), but we believe implicitly that the involvement of interests was substantial and that the disclosure provisions have shed considerable light on the process as it really is. Those who support the campaign reform law also argue that as long as there is disclosure—as long as voters know who is supporting whom—they can make an informed choice and that is the best a democracy can offer. Elizabeth Drew's thesis that things are now in particularly bad straits, although subject to considerable controversy among scholars and journalists, reflects the fear of interests that has characterized American political life from the very beginning. It may be naive, but it is a deeply-held attitude which periodically emerges in a wave of political reform that shoves against the tide of interest-based politics.

An Imbalance of Power.   The charge of intentional or unintentional corruption aside, then, what else makes interests discredible? Power is the most important element. We fear those interests which have the capacity to exercise too much power, whether they act above board or not. We have always feared business interests more than any other because they have the capacity to spend more money than anyone else. The antitrust laws of the Progressive Era are representative of the consistency of our attitudes in expecting public power to control private power.

Sometimes the fear is imbedded in the balance of powers among interests, such as labor's fear of business and vice versa. Edwin M. Epstein, a labor scholar at the University of California at Berkeley, has frequently made the point that the bulk of campaign reform legislation has come as a response by labor to business, or, more specifically, as an overreaction to the unintended consequences of the previous reform which appeared to alter the balance in favor of business. One example of this fear occurred in 1978 when organized labor tried to come to grips with the emergence in electoral politics of corporate PACs.

Although the campaign law, as interpreted by the Federal Election Commission, made provision for corporate giving several years before, it had taken some time to seep down to the institutional level of the corporations themselves. Whereas there were 150 corporate PACs in 1976, there were 776 in 1978. One major impetus to the spurt was the controversial *SunPac* decision (from the Sun Oil Company) made by the Federal Election Commission in 1975, which permitted corporate PACs to solicit contributions from their employees (instead of just their stockholders). Congress limited solicitations from blue collar workers the next year, but the decision opened up what is today *the* major source of corporate PAC funding: white collar workers.

Trade association PACs grew from a little over 300 to 513 in that same two-year period, from 1976 to 1978. Labor, on the other hand, had increased from 201 to 263 PACs and saw itself severely limited in both the number of PACs it could establish and the money it could raise from its membership.[5]

In 1977, the building trades were trying to pass legislation in Congress on common situs picketing. The legislation came to be viewed as a test case for the entire labor movement, perhaps because the building trades did have one important advantage: unlike the large industrial unions that tend to be concentrated in a few states, the construction workers were everywhere and each local had the capacity to influence its representative in Congress. The Business Roundtable, an influential organization made up of the heads of major corporations, came out against the legislation, along with several other business groups. Democratic members of Congress, most of whom were heavily supported by labor, got nervous and bowed to the pressure (the campaign law and its consequences for fund raising being new to everyone including incumbent congressmen). Some of those involved in the Roundtable debate at the time were surprised because they expected to use their position as a point from which to negotiate, not as a demand in itself.

With the defeat of the legislation, COPE (The Committee on Political Education of the AFL–CIO) decided to teach the Democrats a lesson by withholding its support from what were termed the "quasi-marginals," that is, those members of Congress who came from marginal districts who were likely to be re-elected, but who were hardly secure in their seats.

The COPE strategy left the targeted Democrats in a difficult position. If they could not raise money from labor, they would have to turn to business; if they turned to business, they would lose the support of labor. On the other hand, it also left labor between a rock and a hard place. By denying their support to the Democratic incumbents, they forced many to appeal to business to make up the difference, thereby causing a probable shift in loyalties.

In accordance with their policy, labor contributions to the quasi-marginals declined by 25 percent from the 1976 level, and they also declined in proportion to total committee contributions. Only 44 percent of the committee money came from labor in the end, compared to 57 percent in 1976, and much of that money came late in the campaign, after the chastened candidates and the Democratic party put as much pressure as they could on the unions.[6]

It is instructive for our purposes to note that the quasi-marginals turned to the Democratic party for help in 1978, and were given as much aid as the party could then muster. A Democratic incumbent could expect to receive $2,600 for House races in 1978; this particular group received $7,000.[7]

In 1984, corporate PACs numbered 1,763; trade association PACs totaled 684; and labor PACs reached 430.[8] The balance of power these figures suggest is not as pro-Republican as one might guess. Both corporate and trade association giving patterns tend to be less partisan than labor, which gives over 90 percent of its funds to Democrats. The single largest group of recipients of funds from these PACs are incumbents, and since there are more Democratic incumbents than Republicans in office, it was a lesson the GOP learned the hard way when it set about organizing corporate PACs in 1976, only to find out that they gave more to Democrats. In 1978, the Republican National Committee encouraged corporate PACs to reserve a quarter of their contributions for "risk" candidates (that is, Republican challengers), which they did, and which somewhat helped alter the incumbent bias.

It is the pursuit of a safe strategy that prompts business to give to incumbents. Above all, a corporate PAC wants to stay out of trouble. As a result, it is usually easier to give to anyone who asks, especially if he or she stands a chance of winning election. The cost of saying "no" appears to outweigh the benefit of political preference.

Another Republican concern about the balance of powers following Watergate grew out of the realization that many of their top political operatives had been tainted by the 1972 election and had dropped out of politics. This was particularly true of those based in Washington. Without their guidance, and fearful of what was believed to be labor's growing influence, several Republican leaders helped generate a number of new organizations to supplement the party the way labor helps the Democrats. Included in the group are such New Right organizations as the National Conservative Political Action Committee (NCPAC), the Committee for the Survival of a Free Congress, Americans for Change, Americans for an Effective Presidency, and the Fund for a Conservative Majority. The New Right does spend as much as labor, and supports Republicans as labor supports Democrats, but it is an uneasy ally for the Republican party.

Uncertain, Unaccountable Behavior: The Independent Spenders. Although many lessons could be learned from these stories about the relationship between interests and parties, our purpose in retelling it here is to note the fear both business and labor political activity can generate. We are not suggesting the fear is unwarranted, only that it is constant. There are other fears we hold about the influence of interests in electoral politics. One, of course, is that we fear those we do not understand, and we frequently do not understand those who do not agree with us. If we have an enemy and we do not know what that enemy is doing, we are apt to ascribe all sorts of evil things to them. Even if we know what they are doing, we may fear them because their actions do not conform to our expectations. The independent spending by groups of the New Right which has become so controversial in the past several years is a perfect case in point.

Independent expenditures, according to the law, are those expenditures made by individuals or groups advocating the election or defeat of an issue or a candidate, without consultation with either the candidate or his campaign committee. There is no limit on how much can be spent. The Supreme Court held in *Buckley* v. *Valeo* that the First Amendment right of free speech is curtailed if one cannot communicate, and money is equated with communication in our technological society. Although the Court decision was intended to preserve the rights of local citizens groups, it was of more benefit to those groups in Washington that did the vast bulk of independent spending. Most of these groups advocated conservative causes or were set up to balance the influence of labor. There has been some spending on the left, by such groups as People for the American Way, but most of that has come in response to the spending on the conservative side and is insignificant in contrast.

In the 1980 presidential campaign, $13.7 million was spent independently. Five conservative groups spent more than $10 million of the total amount advocating the election of Ronald Reagan: NCPAC, Americans for an Effective Presidency, The Congressional Club (headed by Jesse Helms and also known as The Congressional Club of North Carolina), the Fund for a Conservative Majority and Americans for Change. In 1984, $18.5 million was spent independently, $16.5 million at the presidential level, and $14.6 million of that by the New Right groups.[9]

It is a great deal of money, particularly in an election that is supposed to be evenly balanced financially because of public funding. The capacity of these groups, or of any group, to raise that money, largely through small donations, and to spend it as it sees fit without the limitations imposed on campaigns or parties, would give campaign managers pause even if the groups were not controversial in their own right. As it happens, the presidential election is probably the most impervious to independent spending because of the tremendous visibility it has.

NCPAC, which is the most sophisticated and professional of the conservative groups, led the way to what appears to be a successful campaign against liberal senators by targeting resources (and encouraging other, sometimes less responsible and usually less professional, groups to do the same) in their re-election campaigns, which, at a minimum, emphasized the liberalness of their records, and at a maximum, distorted their records entirely. It is difficult to prove the independent spending made a difference in the outcome of the elections, but by the same token, it would be foolish to conclude it was irrelevant.[10]

Sometimes it is not so much the money spent as the fear of money that can give independent spending groups their power. In 1984, NCPAC filmed a television ad with Ann Gorsuch, former director of the Environmental Protection Agency in the Reagan administration, attacking the Democratic vice-presidential nominee, Geraldine Ferraro. NCPAC's major expense was funding the ad—it achieved much of its purpose by drawing considerable press commentary without ever appearing on the air. On the other side of the spectrum, The Women's Trust was trying to do the same thing with radio ads aimed at increasing the "gender gap" which would be sufficiently controversial to gain them free media. In both instances, the object was to provoke discussion and strengthen their proponents at relatively little cost.

If any conclusion can be drawn, it is probably that independent spending is likely to have a greater impact on elections in which the visibility (and voter interest) is relatively low because it provides information where information is at minimum. While independent spending has predominated at the presidential level just because of the high visibility, most politicians at all levels fear the unknown and unaccountable nature of the groups and the unpredictable things they might say.

Independent spending usually takes the form of an advertisement in the electronic or print media, a direct mail letter, or the printing of pamphlets. The law requires that groups or individuals who engage in such spending register with the Federal Election Commission and report their source of income and their expenditures. Sometimes the ads become a battle between interests as when People for the American Way bought full-page newspaper ads on the issue of religion and politics in the 1984 election. The ad, appearing several weeks before the general election, showed a tablet inscribed with the words "Thou shalt not mix Church and State," and a citation at the bottom of "The Constitution. Chapter 1, Verse: 1." On the side, the ad ran quotes from several fundamentalists such as that by Moral Majority founder Jerry Falwell: "The idea that religion and politics don't mix was invented by the Devil to keep Christians from running their own country." It followed with an argument against that position and included a form for readers to send money to support the campaign or obtain a free pamphlet on "ten rules for maintaining the separation of church and state."[11]

What makes independent spending controversial is not the debate waged between groups like the Moral Majority and People for the American Way; at least not when the debate is carried out in direct dialogue with each other. There have been three principal objections raised, and a number of "minor" objections.

The first objection is that the independent spenders are less constrained than candidates or parties: they can spend as much as they want; they can say whatever they want. Several years ago, John (Terry) Dolan, the director of NCPAC, made one of the most dramatic statements about the dangers inherent in independent spending:

> Groups like ours are potentially very dangerous to the political process. We could be a menace, yes sir. The independent expenditure groups, for example, could amass this great amount of money and defeat the point

of accountability in politics. We could say whatever we want about an opponent of a Senator Smith and the Senator would not have to say anything. A group like ours could lie through its teeth and the candidate it helps stays clean.[12]

If voters decide that they were misled through an ad or a letter paid for by an independent spender, they cannot hold anyone accountable when the next election rolls around in the way they could, in theory at least, hold an office holder accountable for not keeping campaign promises.

A second major objection is that the groups that rely on independent expenditures as their major political activity, raise their funds through appeals that are designed to intensify conflicts. Most of the money comes from direct mail solicitations to small donors. The motivation for them to give their money is moral satisfaction, in contrast to the motivation of the large donor who expects access to a candidate in return for his gift. The issues you are likely to feel strongly about are usually issues in which your position is in the minority: why else would you care? Being in the majority tends to confer a sense of satisfaction because you know your views will dominate.

The process of whipping up the population, of appealing to the dissatisfied, may have long-term negative consequences for the stability of the political system. For all the debate about increasing or decreasing participation, an important characteristic of involvement has been one's social/economic standing: The higher one stands, the more likely one is to participate; the lower down one is on society's ladder, the lower one's sense of personal efficacy (the belief that participation will make a difference), the less faith one has in the system as a whole, and the less likely one is to participate. The direct mail appeals of these groups are often directed at those who are (or can be) frustrated by the system and have, therefore, less of a commitment to it. By appealing to the fringes, the independent spenders are running the risk of raising expectations that cannot be fulfilled.

This argument is generally applied to the conservative groups of the New Right which do the bulk of the independent spending. It does not hold as true for the groups on the left whose appeals are directed at a wealthier population. Still, even with the greater level of education characteristic of liberals in contrast to conservatives, as long as the appeals are based on minority positions, and as long as they are directed at touching a moral quality, they are divisive on both sides of the spectrum and they make the political debate less consensual than it otherwise might be.

The third major objection is probably of greater concern to campaign managers than anyone else, but it does concern the substance of elections. When someone runs for office, he or she must make a decision about the nature of the candidacy and what kind of choice the campaign will offer. Although very little of that rational strategy may seep down to the voting booth, some will, and most voters will be aware of the broad themes in the election.

In 1980, when one of the authors was managing the bid of John Connally for the Republican presidential nomination, a man from Texas, eager to support Connally despite the apparent weaknesses in his campaign strategy, took out ads in newspapers in Texas and Iowa explaining the real merits of Connally's candidacy—the man Big Business wanted in the White House. As it turned out, however, that particular image of the former Texas governor was one the campaign was hoping to play down in the public's mind.

Campaigns are temporary organizations which operate under extreme pressure and great uncertainty in the best of circumstances. Everyone in the campaign, from the national staff on down to the local party or candidate committee, has their own ideas of what it will take to turn the election around for the candidate, and what will make their contributions to the campaign sufficiently important. There is always a battle for power within the campaign organization as well as for the office sought. Sophisticated marketing strategies, based on extensive research and polling are part of the process, and having a "friend" blow that strategy out of the water is just as damaging as having someone like NPAC's Terry Dolan for an enemy. At least an enemy can be labeled, and even if his charges cannot be entirely overcome, almost every campaign under siege by independent spenders has been able to use the attack to raise money from supporters.

One effort to discourage independent spending in the 1984 election, undertaken by several campaigns, was to call a meeting of the groups likely to undertake such spending early on in the campaign season. The campaign strategy was explained by the candidate's staff and at the end of the presentation it was explained to the participants that since they were there and since they were now informed about the strategy, they would be prohibited by law from making independent expenditures because they could no longer consider themselves independent. As the law becomes better understood by all the participants, and particularly as the independent groups become more sophisticated, it is likely they would not be so easily lured into such a meeting, but it does reflect the anxiety campaign managers hold about the tactic.

On the other side, of course, as each election cycle passes, many of the groups that engage in independent spending grow more sophisticated and professional. In fact, they often hire the same professionals to do their media that the campaigns employ. Independent strategies may mirror campaign strategies. It does not take much to pick up on what candidates want to project about themselves and help them get a wider audience.

There are two objections to independent spending that are directed at more abstract levels: that the active participation by single issue groups in election campaigns threatens concepts of accountability, even if their message is accurate; and that participation by third parties who are not contesting office and, therefore, appear to have little to gain by the outcome, affects opinion formation in an unfair, or inappropriate, manner.

As we have already noted, the first issue of accountability has to do with the opportunity voters have to "throw the rascal out" if they conclude he or she has not kept promises. But accountability through representative government is not a positive value to these single issue groups; it is actually hostile to their perception of how the system ought to work. According to the executive director of one of the major conservative groups:

> Independent expenditures are for people who are forced to deal with an antiquated political situation that doesn't deal with the real political system that exists today. The geographic precincts of the '30s and '40s

are impotent. Now we have social precincts. [Because] they are geographic they [the people] aren't included in the representation. They are disenfranchised people who have little interest in their communities—except for the smaller communities. They are more responsive to being represented by their social precincts than by their geographic precincts.[13]

The idea of the irrelevance of accountability by elected representatives is in sharp contrast to James Madison's argument in his Federalist Paper no. 10 that representation is the best defense against uncontrolled battle among the interests. Madison further states that elected representation is characteristic of republics as opposed to pure democracies which require direct participation in decision making by citizens. Representation is best suited to large societies because the size and the inevitable differences of opinion combine to assure the greatest stability, the greatest tendency toward compromise, and the least likelihood that the passions of a single group or interest will override the whole.[14]

The single issue groups seek to combine the minorities and target their strength in selected congressional districts in such a way as to make a majority in a given election district. A slightly different approach was used when a number of groups raised money nationally for the purpose of opposing Senator Edward M. Kennedy's re-election campaign in Massachusetts but spent it in other states where the chances of defeating a liberal were greater. This tactic is both a tyranny of the minority and a breakdown in the nature of representation because the majority in the district cannot hold the minority accountable. It is a tactic that is growing in use by interests on all sides of the spectrum and by groups that contribute to campaigns as well as those who make independent expenditures. One wonders, for instance, what the campaign for the Senate in North Carolina between Jesse Helms and Jim Hunt would have been like in 1984 without the massive infusion of funds to both candidates from all across the country.

The question of influence in opinion formation undoubtedly requires some study, but reason would suggest that groups have a different impact than candidates. We tend to take what a candidate says in the course of a campaign with a grain of salt; we have grown accustomed to candidates accusing each other of sins of great and momentous importance. A noncandidate, however, someone who is not contesting office, is in a different situation.

When we are confronted with opposing opinions, we usually draw our own conclusions by balancing the views; we weigh the credibility of each side. A neutral party in such a balancing, someone who has nothing to gain by the outcome, carries greater weight in our judgement just because he has nothing to gain. Independent spenders, therefore, may carry more weight than either of the candidates in an election because they are not running for office.

Independent spending is a relatively new technique and most of the organizations that have been involved in electoral politics have already developed their repertoire of campaign activities. It would be atypical of any organization to explore unknown waters if the old ways sufficed. Independent spending, therefore, has become more of a tool for the newer groups because they were not bound to the old ways of doing things, and because it is eminently suited to their needs as organizations and the resources they have to employ.

Despite the controversy, some of which is due to technique and some to those who employ it, independent spending has an inconclusive record when it comes to electoral outcomes. Most money is raised and spent at the presidential level because of the visibility of the race and the opportunity it provides to raise money nationally, although it doubled at the congressional level from 1980 to 1984. The visibility of the presidential race also lessens the impact of anybody's spending, not that the old dictum that more is more no longer applies: Republicans can significantly outspend Democrats and only a fool would conclude it would not matter. It is just that we are not sure how it matters because each individual voter's decision is complex and somewhat unpredictable.

Controversy aside, then, how does independent spending affect the parties in their control over elections? Thus far, at least, it does not appear to have had much impact on the parties at all, although it may have had an impact on the outcome of some elections. Most of it has been directed at candidates and issues, not the parties per se, and most of it has been directed in campaigns of high visibility where it is likely to have the least effect. NCPAC began a series of anti-Democratic ads in the 1984 campaign, but they may be substantively no different than party advertising, and the Federal Election Commission was completely divided (along partisan lines) as to whether or not the ads were permissable under the law.

The Relationship between Interest Groups and Parties

Interest groups and parties differ in size and scope. They have different objectives: one the control of government; the other control of policy in a specific area. One seeks to encompass the widest possible coalition, the other would lose its identity and purpose for existence if it was anything but alone. According to E. E. Schattschneider, the central fact of a free society relates to the contagiousness of conflict: "The outcome of all conflict is determined by the *scope* of its contagion. . . . Every change in the number of participants, every increase or every reduction in the number of participants affects the result. . . . Every change in the scope of conflict has a bias; it is partisan in nature. That is, it must be assumed that every change in the number of participants is about something, that the newcomers have sympathies or antipathies that make it possible to involve them."[15] Interests are not usually interested in widening the scope of conflict because their power to control the outcome declines; parties require broad coalitions and, therefore, do seek to broaden the participation.

These characteristics aside, however, the question remains of whether or not the changes in American political life in the past few years have not altered the capacity of interest groups to become competitive with the parties. Is the party system in danger of a take-over by an interest or a group of interests? Have the changes in communication technology and campaign finance law made the parties less important and the interests more important?

THE NATURE OF A THREAT

Interest groups raise money, support (and oppose) candidates, seek to influence party platforms, and communicate directly and indirectly with citizens. Some groups have large membership organizations with chapters at the national, state, and local levels.

Some interests are clearly better financed and better organized than the political parties but they do not exist in the mutually-exclusive environment of a two-party system which always structures decisions as a choice between one or the other party. There are always many interests and many degrees of intensity. There have been occasions when an interest has striven to take over a party, as when the Moral Majority decided to take over the Republican party in Alaska a few years ago because the incumbent political leaders were not sufficiently conservative. But party take-overs are not uncommon and used to happen almost every four years when a maverick presidential candidate (often representing a controversial issue position, as when Robert F. Kennedy and Eugene McCarthy ran for the Democratic nomination in 1968 as peace candidates) encourages supporters to gain control of the local party apparatus to assure representation at the nominating conventions. The argument is often made that these periodic raids on local party leadership are what make the parties vital and representative from one political period to the next.

There is a difference, however, between a threat to the status quo of party leadership within the party and a threat to the party per se. A threat to the party would occur if the party was in danger of being replaced (as when the Republicans replaced the Whigs in the last century), or if the party was in danger of losing some, or all, of its functions: controlling nominations, contesting elections, or being the vehicle for broad-based coalitions which would influence government.

Third Parties.   Although we live in a two-party system, minority parties are not unknown and we have come to recognize the special role they play in acting as a kind of safety valve when issues become too controversial for the major parties to handle. Typically, a third party will emerge and give voice to the intensely held view of a minority, or a coalition of minorities. Names such as Anti-Masons, Free Soilers, Greenbacks, Prohibitionists, and States' Righters reflect their origins in people who believed so strongly in their cause they would use it as a banner to attract like-minded dissidents from the major parties. That none have succeeded in winning a major office or replacing a major party since the Republican victory more than a century ago is due as

much to the complication of ballot access in each of the states as
it is to the basic stability of the two-party system. But the point is
that none have succeeded.

One reason third parties today find it difficult to establish themselves is structural: the laws differ widely from state to state and
all of them are designed to make minority party bids difficult. The
State of Florida, for instance, requires a minority party to submit
a petition signed by 3 percent of the registered voters to get on the
ballot. The percentage is greater than the number of voters in any
given state legislative district and equal to approximately 60 percent of a congressional district. The campaign finance law is also
written to encourage the major parties and discourage fringe candidacies. In 1976, when the law first went into effect, Ellen McCor-
mick ran for the presidency on a pro-life ticket, and congressional
law makers began to worry that the public finance regulations were
too much of an incentive. The fear turned out to be relatively
groundless, but the law was rewritten in 1979 to provide more
support for the two major parties. Even with the $7 million of
public funds available to John Anderson to run for the presidency
in 1984, the difficulty of creating the party he needed to have in
order to accept the money was a major, perhaps *the* major, deter-
rent to the former Illinois congressman, who had done relatively
well in the 1980 race.

But the main difficulty minority parties have in becoming electorally competitive is that ideas that are too controversial in one
election are often found to be more acceptable in the next (the
pro-life position being a prime example). It is not so much the
activity of the minority party as it is the desire of the majority party
to subsume into it that issue and the energy its advocates provide.
How an issue becomes acceptable to the established party is undoubtedly a complex process, but the key elements would include
the passage of time, visibility and acceptance in public opinions
polls and in the media, and some movement toward compromise
so that opponents will become less fearful and proponents become
less strident. The major party then drains off the minority party
support and the minority party disappears.

Not all minority parties represent the frustrations of an immediate issue. The Communist and Socialist parties represent political

ideologies whose supporters believe they will eventually triumph but do not expect to do much more than give visibility to their cause in any given election. The point can be made of them, as well as issue parties, that as long as legislatures are structured in a partisan fashion, and as long as single member district voting exists, incumbents will be loathe to lose their seniority within the legislature by switching parties, and candidates of minority parties would have to completely replace one of the major parties in a district to win election. Presidential candidacies offer wider opportunities for amassing support and giving visibility to an issue, but are far less likely to sufficiently overcome a major party to win election.

Control of Nominations.   There are two ways the parties have of influencing nominations: control over the ballot, which is to say that a candidate for office usually must run under a party label in order to have his or her name printed on the ballot (unless they run as an independent, which is often a much more complicated procedure); and the party leadership can be influential in determining who will run by actively recruiting the candidate, by providing substantial support in organization and other resources, and by lending its name to a preferred candidate in a primary fight. The most direct influence, of course, is a decision made by a party committee or convention.

An interest group seeking to determine the outcome of a nomination must either run its candidate as an independent, as a candidate among a host of others in a primary battle, or seek to establish a party in its own name. The AFL-CIO endorsement of Walter Mondale early in the presidential selection process of 1984 was an interesting case in point of the strengths and weaknesses of interest group participation in the nominating process.

Ever since the 1972 campaign when George McGovern was the Democratic nominee, labor's influence had been markedly uninspired. To say that McGovern was not their candidate would be a great understatement. In a period of intense divisiveness over the Vietnam War and the bitter years of the 1960s and the War on Poverty which pitted the lower class against the lower middle class, Senator McGovern represented all of the factions within the Democratic party that labor abhored. His selection as the nominee followed an extensive primary season, complicated by new rules written under McGovern's leadership. Although AFL-CIO leadership made some efforts during the general election to support the candidate, defections among the membership accounted for much of the Nixon landslide in November.

Labor lost out again in 1976 when Jimmy Carter captured the nomination as an outsider who was able to build his own organization in the primaries, making good use of the rules and the number of primaries as had McGovern before him. In 1980, the battle between the incumbent Carter and Senator Edward M. Kennedy caught labor again without a decisive role in the election.

A change in labor's leadership from George Meaney to Lane Kirkland also meant a change in emphasis. To Meaney, labor's strength lay in collective bargaining, but Kirkland believed more strongly in political action. Although he assumed the presidency of the AFL-CIO before 1980, it was not until the 1984 election that Kirkland was strong enough to change the tradition and intervene more actively in the nominating process.

Seeking to back a candidate who could win the general election and carry the backing of labor's membership, the AFL-CIO endorsed Walter Mondale before the first caucus or primary was ever held. Mondale was the frontrunner at the time, followed by John Glenn of Ohio. Other candidates did not seem likely to be much in the running. Although media interviews suggested that most union members did not feel especially strongly about Mondale, neither was there much opposition. The sense of the meeting when the endorsement was made was that labor needed to make a commitment—and follow through on it—in order to make sure the Democratic party remained faithful to labor's interests (the reader will recall the unhappy efforts to punish the "quasi-marginal" congressmen in 1978), and to make sure the Democrats retook the White House in 1984.

When Gary Hart emerged from the pack by coming in a strong second in the Iowa caucus and then winning the New Hampshire primary, labor's early calculation began to seem more of an encumbrance than a blessing. Mondale was labeled the candidate of the interests, and labor was being accused of dragging the party down to defeat because Hart seemed more likely to defeat Reagan than the former vice-president. Hart's early lead in the primaries put as much pressure on the AFL-CIO as it did on the Mondale campaign. It was not until Super Tuesday in March, that Mondale, with as much help as the AFL-CIO could muster, began the road back to frontrunner.

The strength of labor's early endorsement and later commitment went a long way toward making Mondale the Democratic nominee. The weakness turned out to be in the choice of a candidate who was perhaps even less likely to defeat the Republican incumbent than later evidence suggested (although it is highly problematic to think that any Democrat would have defeated Reagan in 1984). Labor's endorsement was thrown at Mondale like an albatross by his opponents inside and outside the party. Even according to Republican strategists, a labor endorsement was never considered a negative until 1984. Some attribute the change to the length of the presidential primary season which helped build up the image of labor as a special interest, and to the many press stories during that time which began with comments that Mondale would not be the frontrunner without the help of the AFL-CIO endorsement. The Mondale staff, in fact, thought the issue was more a press issue than a political issue until the press made it so.[16] The aftermath of the 1984 election will undoubtedly include a re-evaluation by both the party and the labor community.

The lesson for our purposes is not so much the costs it may have had for the Democratic party (which was certainly in bad shape before labor's intervention), but the loss it cost in associating so visibly and so determinately with a candidate in the hopes of influencing the nomination. Organized labor has been an important member of the Democratic coalition since the New Deal. It has never represented a majority of the population, and its prestige has declined considerably in recent years. But even if labor were riding high in the polls, the close affiliation with a candidate can always make that candidate suspect and open to the charge of being too much under its influence. It is a charge that would be made of any interest. It is a charge that can be picked up by the press, by other interests, and certainly by opposing candidates.

Contesting Election. The most controversial role by interest groups of late has been the independent spending, but it should be pointed out that most organizations have eschewed participation in that manner. First, it is controversial and far more visible than a campaign contribution would be. In 1980, no unions and very few corporations made independent expenditures: labor because of its ability to use other avenues to support candidates and the expectations by both those making the decisions within the labor movement and those receiving their support; and corporation PACs because their first order of priority is to avoid controversy. A number of unions did make independent expenditures in 1984, but they remained a minuscule part of labor's efforts in that election campaign.

What about the more traditional role of interests in elections? Some interests are in a better position to make a difference than others; most typically, those which are membership organizations and whose leaders can actually turn out their members to help. It has always been argued that labor's greatest asset is just that: its ability to get union members and their families to register voters, participate in get-out-the-vote drives, and volunteer in campaign headquarters for a host of other political activities. A corporation, in contrast, is hard-pressed to field a sufficient supply of executives and their families for similar work. The National Education Association and the United Automobile Workers have been among the most successful union groups in presidential politics—the former able to rely on the responsibility and credibility of teachers around the country; the latter, on the long history of encouraging political involvement for those who want to move up within the union, and the fact that they are concentrated in often critical primary states.

Business and labor represent the basic economic cleavage between the two major parties (although the balance appears now to be labor against the New Right) but other issues—and the interest groups which represent them—are often more telling in any given election. Political and social issues often have a greater capacity to arouse voter interest, partly because their themes are not so constant and hence can generate passion, and partly because the issues are usually framed in simple terms: war or peace, nuclear freeze or nuclear power, abortion or pro-choice. Economic problems may be clearcut, such as inflation or deficits, but the alternative solutions are complex and not easy to evaluate in the course of a campaign.

Issues, and the basic changes they portend, characteristically play more of a role in presidential than congressional elections because of the visibility and the capacity of a national election to mobilize activists. The single most critical factor in congressional elections tends to be incumbency, which explains why the Democrats have been able to sustain themselves as well as they have, and why the GOP has to go up a very steep hill, indeed, to take control of the House. This is not to say that issues, and the interests who represent them, are not important, but only to put them into a little perspective.

The recent apparently dramatic turns of the Republican party to the right and the Democratic party to the left leaves the impression that they are controlled by the interests, but that may turn out to be a short-term perspective. The parties are in the business of winning elections, which means they must appeal to the broadest possible coalition of support. When they lose, they need to reshuffle the mix, and if voters continue to reject them, they will move to follow the voters. If anyone can be said to dominate the parties, in all probability it would be the uncontrollable voter more than the more predictable interests.

Even when elections can be said to be determined by issues—as many can—the question of whether any particular interest can dominate an issue is more problematic. In the economic issues that have been so important in the past few presidential elections, there are any number of interest groups on each side, but none that could claim to take credit for the victory (or surely not blame for the defeat). If controlling economic interests cannot be identified, what about the more probable social and political issues? The Moral Majority has become an active supporter of Republicans, particularly in the South, as have the supporters of Reverend Jesse Jackson for the Democrats. They may not balance each other out as evenly as James Madison hoped, but they certainly put pressure on each other.

In 1980, the Moral Majority, under the leadership of Reverend Jerry Falwell, were thought to have played a significant role in Reagan's election and in the defeat of the liberal senators targeted by NCPAC and several other conservative groups. In 1984, the same claim was made about the influence of the fundamentalist group in registering voters and getting out their vote. Jesse Jackson's campaign for the Democratic nomination in 1984 galvanized black voters throughout the country and was thought to be something of a counterweight to the Moral Majority. In retrospect, however, it worked the other way around, with the threat of Jackson's success mobilizing both the Moral Majority itself and the Republican party (which spent $10 million in several targeted states in the South on the effort, creating a structure that they expect to serve them well in the future).[17] It does not say a great deal for the decline of racism in America, but the result of the competition was the largest increase in registered voters ever. Each group has claims to register with their respective parties; each group may have been instrumental in electoral outcomes in any given district. And each group faces the same problem with the party: the group has no place else to go.

Despite the fact that Ronald Reagan's first term in the White House was a disappointment to fundamentalist leaders because neither the president nor the party made the issues of concern to the fundamentalist a high priority, the Moral Majority had to come back to Reagan in 1984. The group made a stronger stand during the nominating convention with respect to the platform, but Reagan made clear that he had his own agenda and would not be completely bound by the platform.

Black supporters of the Democratic party have a longer history of commitment, support, and lack of attention. More than 80 percent of registered blacks are Democrats (making them the most consistently Democratic group in the nation), but black leaders are in a difficult position when it comes to bargaining with the party because they cannot bolt to the Republicans, who have little to offer them, without alienating their own constituency. Jackson's innovation was to force the candidates to bargain with him before the nomination was secured. His success was dependent on the fear that if the leaders did not negotiate, his supporters would lose faith with the system and just stay home (and that could be the margin of victory or defeat in a close election). It was a reasonable supposition, given the charismatic and credible campaign he waged during the primary season—a campaign made both probable and improbable by the belief by most Democrats that Jackson was an articulate spokesman who did not stand much of a chance of winning either the nomination or the presidency.

Can the Interests Take Over the Party?

If the nature of our two-party system requires that the coalition for governance be put together before the election, rather than afterwards as is the case in a parliamentary system, clearly the parties must appeal to the interests for their support before the election. The question is how much the parties must give in return for an interest's support. It is our contention that a party/interest group relationship is a two-way street, but the party always has the wider lane.

The economic-based interests of business and labor play a more integral role in the structure because they reflect the basic political cleavage that underlies our two-party system. It gives them great influence in the long run, but they may be at a disadvantage in any given election because of negative public attitudes to their consistent strength, or because other issues are capable of capturing the emotions of the moment. The parties always trade with the economic interests, but because the balance of power between the interests and between the parties is finely crafted and maintained, they are sure to check each other at almost every turn. Economic policy generally inches along. The times we have come close to changes in the balance can be recalled easily: the New Deal, which forged a new balance; and the effort by supply side economists in the early years of the Reagan administration, which did make moderate gains. We are not suggesting these gains are insignificant, only that they are unusual.

The interests that are not part of the existing balance of power are the interests that can endanger that balance. The interest most likely (or at least most recently) to arouse enough support to affect the balance are those associated with the issues of war and peace, the environment, civil rights, and questions of morality (abortion, prayer, sexual preference, and so on) The advocates of these issues may come from both parties, but their efforts will be concentrated within the party most likely to be responsive. Sometimes the most responsive party will be the one that is out of power. Sometimes the most responsive party will be the one in the minority, even if it is in power, because it hopes to create a new partisan alignment.

The association, whatever it is, is bound only fortuitously to what we loosely describe as the party's ideology. The Republican party was the main supporter of the Equal Rights Amendment since its introduction more than a half century ago. That it dropped its support in 1980 had more to do with the opportunity to pick up new partisans and the mobilization of the anti-ERA activists who won seats to the 1980 campaign as supporters of Ronald Reagan than it did with Republican philosophy. Did that constitute a take over of the party? Yes, to the extent that it changed the Republican party platform and led to the resignation of some party leaders. It did not lead to a significant shift of position by incumbent Republican office holders who are more dependent on their constituents for election (and the majority of the population favors passage of the ERA). It did lead to the emergence (and success) of anti-ERA candidates in those parts of the country where the Amendment is unpopular.

For many years, the Democratic party was an uneasy mix of liberals in the North and conservatives in the South. It got by because it kept the most divisive issues off the national agenda. The coalition began to fall apart when civil rights became part of national Democratic policy. The Republicans picked up the disaffected Democrats in the South, and it is among this group that opponents of the ERA and abortion are most consistently found.

The Republican party may rise or fall in some elections on the ERA and abortion issues in the next few years. New regions of the country may be added to the Republican strongholds. The GOP may become the majority party. But what will happen to the issues that generated (or at least accompanied) this shift? In all probability, as long as the majority of the population remains favorable toward the ERA and toward the availability of abortions, the Republican party will do very little about it. It will give voice to the opponents. It will encourage candidates who can win on those issues. It will accommodate itself to whatever it takes to win office and accept the inconsistencies among the different regions of the country. But if it loses elections because its candidates took an unpopular position, it will support more moderate candidates. It will accept the support of an interest—any interest—as long as that issue garners support, and it will back away when the cost is too great. The test is an election, or sometimes several elections. But no demands can be made upon the party by anyone, or any combination of persons or groups, if that demand clearly goes against the wishes of the majority of voters.

The moral issues are the most difficult for a party to accept, and once accepted, to deflect. The genius of the parties is their capacity to bring about compromise, to evoke consensus. The moral issues are inherently rigid. It is not just a question of organizational politics in which the leadership cannot afford to give ground lest it lose constituency support. It is built into the substance of the issue: if abortion is murder, there is no middle ground. Neither is there a middle ground if no abortion threatens the life and well-being of a woman.

The worst case—the one the parties failed most dramatically—led to the Civil War. Obviously, there were serious economic and political contributing factors, but the parties were incapable of sustaining the compromises worked out in the 1850s, and the Republican party, born out of the fervor of the antislavery movement, replaced the Whigs and we went to war with ourselves. There is little likelihood of war today (the thought did not seem so far fetched in the late 1960s and early 1970s over civil rights or the peace movement), but the prospect may help us put the relationship between the parties and the interests into perspective.

First, the interests cannot act in the political arena alone: they cannot nominate candidates for office because ballot access is under state and party control and because they are always minorities; they cannot control the structure of legislative organization (that is, the election of speakers and committee chairpersons, which is a party function); and they cannot control the votes of elected officials if the constituencies of those officials oppose them.

If the interests cannot act alone, then they must combine, but if they combine they must have something to offer each other and trades of that sort must at some point mean compromise. At that point, a combination of interests will be like a party. The significant difference between such a coalition and a party will be the legal structure and function of the parties in elections.

Many political scientists believe that the underlying reason for the parties survival is because of the duality of their nature. They do not have to be strong organizationally if they are balanced. They do not have to be coherent as long as the election reduces the option to a simple choice: one party or the other. According to E. E. Schattschneider, that simplification gives focus to the political world and enables us to find a place for ourselves in that world.[18] As long as interests are multiple, they cannot simplify. As long as our lives are complex, we will identify with many interests, and they may not all fall within one coalition.

The parties may not be eternal, but they are an integral part of our political system. They feed on interests which help them expand their base in any given election. Elections are frequently determined by a single overriding issue, and the interests represented in that issue may be seen to have dominated the parties. But each election cycle presents a different set of issues, because the first issue was resolved, or we just got bored with it. Only the party goes on from one election to the next.

We may never find consensus on abortion. We are still trying to move toward consensus on civil rights. The more important question may be not who dominates, but where and how the debate is held. The Constitution provides the skeletal structure of elections; the parties provide the options for those elections; the interests are the food for debate. But the diet is the most changing part of the entire scheme. The debate is always held within the parties which is the final arbiter on how it will be presented as a choice to the voters.

6

That Elusive Arbiter:
The Voter

THUS FAR, we have avoided one of the most important criteria used to demonstrate the decline of the parties: the attitude of the voters. The decline in partisan identification from the time we began measuring such things (in the early 1950s) through the beginning of the 1980s has been the best argument for demonstrating the weak, ineffective party system. Bad news always travels faster than good news, or at least gets bigger headlines, and there does not seem to be as much to-do about the increase in partisan identification revealed in the endless polling of the last election.

Partisan identification in the mid-1980s is about on a par with what it was in 1952: approximately three-quarters of the population will respond, when pressed, to a party preference. The decline in strong partisan identifiers has been matched by an increase in those who describe themselves as independent, but who "lean" toward one or the other of the two major parties, and over the years we have learned that "leaners" vote the same way as identifiers. In the last few years, the percentage of "strong identifiers" has risen, particularly in the Republican party which reached a nadir in 1974 of 7 percent and more than doubled that to 18 percent in 1984, putting it higher than it was in 1952.

According to a Harris Survey published after the 1984 election, Republican identifiers increased from 26 to 34 percent, and Democrats increased from 41 to 42 percent (after a low of 38 percent in 1980). Self-identified independents dropped from 28 to 20 percent.[1]

The ups and downs of party popularity is central to conceptions of stability. Political theorists point to it when speaking about the democracy writ large; politicians rely upon it when calculating their chances in elections. Our purpose in this chapter is twofold: to explore the nature of partisanship, particularly in terms of voting behavior; and to build a case for the argument that the decline was due, at least in part, to the weakness of the party structure. Or, put another way, that the recent increase has been fostered by the energy and appeals coming from a stronger party organization.

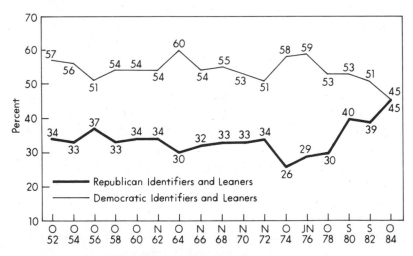

FIG. 6-1

Distribution of Party Identification in the United States
1952–1984

NOTE: Data supplied by Market Opinion Research, based in part on the studies undertaken by the Center for Political Studies, University of Michigan.

THE NATURE OF PARTISANSHIP

Partisanship, or at least political attitudes, are important to us in ways that transcend the issues or candidate choice in any given election. Political attitudes are ways of anchoring ourselves. They identify our friends and our enemies. They give us a place in the society, and they give the society a meaning and a purpose. Political attitudes come very early and are not likely to change unless there are major political upheavals in the world at large, or unless we ourselves go through major social changes and want to adopt the attitudes of those with whom we associate. Upwardly mobile Democrats moving to the suburbs in the 1950s often became Republicans, for instance.

Partisanship means a loyalty to a set of ideas and a group of people. Once the loyalty is established, it helps an individual judge which other ideas and other people are of value and which are to be considered wrong or antagonistic. Most issues do not generate sufficient intensity to overcome the underlying loyalty. Those issues that do break through partisan interpretation may cause a change of partisanship or may lead only to a dissonance on that particular subject. Support of the Equal Rights Amendment among Republicans following the 1980 national convention which disavowed it would be one example; another, would be the Vietnam War for both parties. Issues such as war and peace or economic stability are capable of leading to a shift in partisanship and a realignment of the power of the political parties. Deep social issues such as civil rights are also potentially realigning issues.

The desire to be in step with the party (and all that the party comes to mean in terms of being in step with like-minded persons) often leads to a individual's forming an opinion because it is the party's position. It can also lead an individual into believing that his or her opinions are identical with the party's even when they are not.

The desire for conformity, or perhaps put more accurately, the desire to reduce dissonance, is undoubtedly a strong motivator, but it is helped by the complexity of politics and communication, which often leaves an individual in the dark about his party's views. Needless to say, if the issue is sufficiently controversial as to war-

rant strong statements by party leaders, the probability of igno-
rance declines, but it does not entirely destroy the capacity to find
points of commonality and lessen the difference in the mind of the
individual.

The most important influence in the development of partisanship
is the family. Generation gaps notwithstanding, the attitudes we
learn as children from both parents about authority and social
responsibility are surprisingly durable. Education, peer groups,
and our own experience and place in the world are also influential
in the development of political attitudes.

Typically, the first big political event an individual becomes
aware of (an assassination, major depression, the end or beginning
of war, and so forth), plays an important role in the formation of
that person's political attitudes, confirming or denying the basic
beliefs developed in the family. Another major factor in political
behavior is age and where one is in the life cycle. Young people,
with few attachments to the community in the form of family or
home ownership, for example, are less likely to vote than those who
are older. Voting is an act that reinforces itself, both in going to
the polls and in developing party attachments. It is a habit that
comes with age and the experience of participating in one election
after another. Once you say to yourself that you are a Republican
or a Democrat, you tend to think of yourself that way.

All of these influences combine to make absolute independence
from partisan influence difficult to sustain. Every issue is capable
of touching our sense of values. Every issue is subject to interpretation or else it is not likely to become a political question in the first
place. No one, for instance, favors drunk drivers, but solutions to
the problem will vary tremendously depending on one's sense of
how responsible the government or the individual citizen ought to
be in dealing with the problem.

The pressures for partisanship notwithstanding, there is a strong
antipartisan tradition in American culture that works against partisan attachments, or at least against acknowledging partisan attachments. It encourages us to think that we are above partisanship
and that we make our decisions in a rational, unbiased manner.
Harry Truman was once asked on the eve of an election how he
planned to vote and he responded that he always votes for "the best

man, and that man is always the Democrat." Pollsters have shown us that most people make similar decisions.

CHANGES IN PARTISANSHIP

It was a fortuitous circumstance that the study of voters began in the 1950s, a period of relative calm in American political life. The majority of the voting population had grown up in an age of strong partisanship and they were not challenged by the times to change their views, with the exception of those who moved to the suburbs. As Norman H. Nie, Sidney Verba, and John R. Petrocik point out in their book, *The Changing American Voter,* written in 1976 as an up-date to the classic *American Voter* by Angus Campbell, Philip E. Converse, Warren E. Miller and Donald E. Stokes, published a decade before in 1964,

> The works of the 1950s uncovered what appeared to be long-term, not easily changeable attitudes. . . . The partisan commitments based on the earlier issues remained . . . and in the absence of other forces, were transmitted to the next generation. Under the circumstances, party seemed all-important, issues unimportant. . . . But when one has the combination of the weakening of older issues, the rise of potent new issues, and a new generation of voters, the stability of party commitments is shattered.[2]

The issues that determined the politics of the 1950s (as much as issues could be said to have determined that period at all) were defined by the New Deal, two decades before. New issues emerged in the 1960s, molding a new generation, altering the attitudes of many in older generations. Typically, however, as Nie, Verba, and Petrocik point out, those most affected were those with the weakest partisan links: the young.[3]

The percentage of strong partisans has been relatively stable over time. There were 22 percent who described themselves that way in October of 1952, and 20 percent who described themselves that way in October of 1984. The fluctuation reached a low of 14 percent in the fall of 1981 and a high of 26 percent in October of 1964. Strong Republicans began at 13 percent in 1952, and reached an all-time high in this period of 18 percent in October of 1984. The GOP low was 7 percent, reached in December of 1974.

The astute observer will be able to correlate the ups and downs with the major political events of presidential elections and the popularity of the nominees as well as with Watergate and the Vietnam era. With the exception of Watergate, which was the most serious political shock to voters in this period, strong partisans have remained relatively stable.

One measure of partisan identification that may be particularly interesting for our purposes is the shift between strong and weak partisan identifiers (we will get to independents shortly). In 1952, both parties had more weak partisans than strong partisan identifiers. Remember, this is at a time when voting analysts described Americans as more motivated by party than by issues when it came to casting their ballots. In 1984, more people were describing themselves as strongly partisan than weakly partisan. The margins were not very great, but the distribution is interesting because it suggests that the parties have come to have more meaning for those who support them.

	1952 (%)	1984 (%)
Democrat		
Strong	22	20
Weak	25	15
Republican		
Strong	13	18
Weak	14	11

We would argue that the large shift in the Republican party reflects greater coherence within the party on the one hand, and perhaps most importantly, a greater capacity to communicate a message about positions on the other. We would argue that a related phenomenon is the increase in the GOP donor base, which now amounts to somewhere between three and a half to four million contributors. Although we do not have comparable figures to measure the increase in donors for the entire national party, the growth of the Republican Congressional Campaign Committee is probably as good an indication as any. It went from a base of 25,000 active contributors in June of 1975 to almost a million and a half in November of 1984.⁴ Fund raisers know that commitment follows money, which suggests an increased sense of participation and identification for those who give, and their family and friends.

INDEPENDENTS

Twenty-one percent of the population described themselves as independents in 1952; 36 percent described themselves so in 1984. There are two classes of independents: those who lean toward the major parties, and those who express no leaning. The "leaners," we have learned, tend to vote the same way partisans vote. If we exclude them for the moment, the proportion of true independents has declined considerably in recent years (ranging from 5 percent in 1952 to 8 percent in 1984). The largest percentage of independents came at the height of Watergate, when 16 percent put themselves into that category in the winter of 1974.

We can look at independents in several ways: as a demonstration of the loss of party credibility; or as a result of an increase in levels of education and social mobility, which may encourage individuals to think of themselves as nonpartisan in their political choices. We can think of the decrease in party identification as a dramatic change in the political world, or we can think of the behavior of voters as more or less the same, with most people still making their judgements about candidates based on their assessments of the parties.

The important question for us is how this weakening of partisan ties affects the strength of the political system. One element of party strength has to do with stability (the institutions of governance: legitimacy, accountability, predictability). Another issue has to do with the alternatives: are parties weaker and interests stronger in the hearts and minds of the voters? Have individual candidates replaced the long-term loyalties of parties and how would that affect the capacity of the voter to sort out the politics of the day without the set of values and cues a party provides?

POLITICAL STABILITY

Voting behavior has become a wonderfully complex field of study for political scientists. It lends itself to debates about methodology and interpretation. It has an air of authority and science about it, revealing the mysteries of vaguely held values and less than consistent behavior. Over the years, it has drawn an interesting and probably accurate picture of how Americans view the political system and how our views change over time.

In the beginning—in the 1950s, when the University of Michigan studies began—issues appeared to be less important than party identification in a voter's calculation of how to cast his ballot. Given the politics of the day, it was not a surprising observation, but it was not until the late 1960s and early 1970s that it became clear to scholars that policy positions had replaced the party as the primary factor in voting decisions for a growing proportion of the population. It was then that the parties were seen to be dying.

It was not until the late 1970s, that some students of the field began to see the importance of parties and issues in making an electoral choice as part of an ebb and flow. Philip Converse and Gregory Markus used the analogy of watching reeds in a shallow pool: if the wind blows to the west, the reeds bend to the west; if it blows to the east, they blow that way. When there is no wind, they stand upright in a "middling" position. "From some points of view the motion is of interest since it tells us which way the wind is blowing at the moment. From some points of view, it is not of great interest, since we know the reeds are not moving in an absolute sense, but are firmly anchored in a fixed position by their roots."[5]

The polarities appear to be divided between parties and interests: one or the other tends to motivate voters. The character of the candidate can also be critical, particularly at the executive levels of government, or in races with enough visibility to make character known, but the field of study has structured the debate principally around the first two elements. It is not our purpose to do a major analysis of voting behavior studies but only to indicate those aspects of the research that affect our theme: what partisanship means to voters; how stronger or weaker parties affect them; and how changes come about.

We accept the notion that parties bend with the wind, waxing stronger in some periods, waning in others. We accept the idea that when the parties are weaker, issues are stronger, although the causal relationship subscribed to by some political scientists must be tempered by the knowledge that political reforms in the first half of the century went a long way toward weakening the parties without much regard to the issues.

Legitimacy. As a first response to the question of stability, let us accept the premise that the parties are durable, but that they do not always play a premier role in the calculation of voters casting ballots. There was an interesting poll result following the 1984 election about first-time voters. Ninety-four percent of the men and 93 percent of the women who described themselves as Republicans voted for Ronald Reagan, which is not a dramatic revelation. Among those who described themselves as Democrats, however, less than three-quarters of the men (72 percent) and just over that (76 percent) of the women voted for Mondale.[6] It may not seem surprising that a quarter of the new Democrats deserted their party's nominee in an election that turned out to be a Reagan landslide, but it does seem a little curious that at the same time they would express a partisan identity at odds with their voting choice. Even accepting the probability that they voted Democratic lower down on the ticket, the expression of partisan identity suggests a set of values and attitudes likely to influence them in a variety of electoral choices.

Seymour Martin Lipset and William Schneider suggest that confidence in a society is due more to political beliefs than sociological factors. They note that extreme ideologues, on both sides of the spectrum, "are below average in confidence," but even more significantly, those who describe themselves as being independent of the political parties "have the lowest confidence in institutions generally." In contrast, Republicans and Democrats have the highest level of confidence, leading Lipset and Schneider to conclude that "general confidence seems to be associated with partisanship per se."[7]

Although Lipset and Schneider do not draw a causal conclusion from their exhaustive study of polling data, noting for instance that declining faith in the legitimacy of the system might lead to a declining faith in the political parties, they do believe that "the relationship between confidence and partisanship suggests that something real is being measured in the general index of confidence, namely a form of institutional trust and identification that applies to political parties as well as to the other twelve institutions regularly tested by NORC [National Opinion Research Center at the University of Chicago]."[8]

In the aftermath of Vietnam and Watergate there was a decline in confidence in all institutions. There are strong indications that the "confidence gap" described by Lipset and Schneider is narrowing in the 1980s, partly as a result of a new generation coming of political age. There are also indications that suggest the political parties either hold their adherents to a faith in the system or that they reflect the faith held in the system in general. The parties are, in other words, central to political trust. It is our view that, as the decade progresses, confidence in the system in general will increase, as will partisanship. Which is the chicken and which is the egg in this process may not matter, but the stronger party we have described may have a strong claim on the causal position (whichever that is).

Accountability. In many respects, accountability is the basis of a democratic system. Most citizens participate in the political life of their town, their state, and their nation solely through the casting of their ballot. Given the limitations of the ballot, the options to express a view on a complex subject are limited. However popular referenda questions may have become in recent years, they will always remain an awkward way to make decisions about the distribution of goods and services because they cannot take account of the nuances of public policy and they cannot measure out a compromise among competing interests. What the ballot promotes—what a yes or no, or a check beside one name requires—is a simple choice and often an evaluation of the performance of the incumbent. What partisanship provides is the opportunity to give that choice an expression of values and to hold those in power collectively accountable.

Holding the party or the incumbent accountable does not require partisan identification. The voter who judges the party in power (whether it is his or her preferred party or not), finds it wanting, and then votes against it is, as they say, "sending a message." Such messages are frequently sent in congressional elections in nonpresidential election years, especially by weak partisans and independents—assuming that the views of most strong partisans will be colored by their partisanship and they will see their party performing adequately (or at least better than the opposition might). The point is that parties are essential to accountability, requiring the electorate to behave in a partisan fashion, regardless of their affiliation, or lack thereof.

V. O. Key, Jr., in his mid-century study of Southern politics, made the observation that the opportunity to hold office holders accountable declines when parties fail to function in the traditional manner, that is, when one party so dominates as to operate as a complex of factions whose membership shifts from election to election in such a way as to prevent voters from holding a group responsible for their actions because the membership in the group constantly changes. Without a party choice, according to Key, there is no accountability.[9]

Parties are not the only element in the political realm held accountable by voters. Just as basic is the accountability of the candidate who must return to his constituency for re-election on the basis of his record in office (assuming there is enough visibility of his record). Although there are clearly occasions when a member of Congress, a governor, and even a president, face the electorate on one particular controversial position or action as the critical issue of the campaign (Woodrow Wilson's campaign for the League of Nations is one example; less lofty, and more frequent, are issues or questions of morality or government corruption), in most cases and in most elections, the record is long and complex, and the attention of the voter is not focused on it, however much the opposition may try. In such circumstances, the voter's recognition of the name of the candidate, his or her ethnic association, race, gender, and partisan affiliation become the basis of the decision on how to vote.

Another argument about accountability is often made by those who comment on the tendency of voters to cast their ballots for the presidential candidate of one party and the congressional candidates of the other. According to political commentator Alan Baron, writing about the 1984 election:

> Instinctively, ticket-splitters wanted to keep New Deal Democrats from running the country . . . and New Right Republicans, from running wild. Few tell "pollsters" they have this in mind. . . . However, polls show [a] strong desire for "having" an independent Congress . . . [candidates] running as "insurance" against GOP did well. And Democrats' jobs under a GOP President are preserving, not creating, programs.
>
> NJ Reagan/Bradley voters were not ex-movie & basketball fans, and didn't confuse Reagan with Roosevelt or Bradley with fellow tax-reformer Jack Kemp. They know Bradley was no Reaganite, and didn't mind at all.[10]

Baron admits his position is controversial, and many of his colleagues do not share his views, but his views are not uncommon and may be right. Whether he is right or not, the view is so commonly heard that it may be something of a self-fulfilling prophesy for at least some voters.

Predictability.   Pollsters and political scientists notwithstanding, it is the politicians who rely most heavily on partisan distribution in their calculations about campaigns: who is with them; who can be persuaded to join. The core support is usually based on strong party identifiers, and everything else depends on the variables of politics, not the least of which is the choice the voter will have between the candidates. A predictor of growing importance is past voting behavior because of the increased ability of the parties to gather and assimilate such information.

The stability of partisan attitudes (regardless of party registration) from election to election is what makes prediction possible. It may not be a necessary part of the maintenance of the American political system, but it is clearly part of the process because the coalitions that define the two major political parties since the New Deal have become quite unstable lately. The Democratic party, which used to be based on organized labor, Catholics (particularly from not highly assimilated European backgrounds), blacks, and Jews, now can rely only on blacks and Jews (the smallest groups of the old coalition) to give the party at least two-thirds of their votes. Even with the tremendous backing the AFL-CIO gave Walter Mondale's candidacy in 1984, only 53 percent of union households voted for him in the election.[11] The GOP, which was known as the party of business and the upper class, can still pretty much rely on those groups, but needs more than their support to win elections; it has been especially effective in the South, which gave it the largest margin of victory in 1984 of 63 percent.[12]

If every group (other than blacks, Jews, and business) is unstable or can be weaned away from their past tendencies, then the system is either in a state of flux—the ever-awaited realignment—or it has become less partisan. But being less partisan, or in this case less predictable, does not mean the parties have become less significant. Every election is won by a coalition of groups and in every election groups must make a choice between the parties. If, from time to time, they choose the other party, it is because that party offers something, or someone, they find more appealing.

This argument may sound like a tautology, noting that partisanship is important because the system is structured by the parties, but it is a point usually overlooked by those who foretell the death of the parties. Even if we enter an era when one-third of the electorate views itself as Republican, one-third Democratic, and one-third Independent, the elimination of a normal majority party does not mean the elimination of partisan choice.

The defection of party identifiers to at least one of the candidates of the other party—ticket splitting—appears to have been on a continuing rise from 1956 (when it was 28 percent of all ballots cast) through 1974, when it reached a recorded high of 56 percent.* The data are not available for the next two elections, but it had declined to 51 percent in 1980.[13] Usually, the defection is in presidential voting, but there has been an increase in ticket splitting at lower ends of the ladder. Presumably, the greater visibility candidates below the presidential level receive because of the media, and their increased ability to communicate to voters through the mail, is part of the reason. Two other possible explanations are that interest groups are making more active endorsements, and less likely, that genre party advertising has indirectly influenced opposing party members who may come to feel better about the other party even if they do not think of themselves as belonging to it.

---

*This figure is higher than that reported in the later study by Ornstein, Mann, Malbin, and Bibby. See page 172.

What is most difficult for analysts of the political process is to sort out what is a true alteration in the system and what is a byproduct of change. Arguments can be made, with ample justification, that the large role played by interests in campaigns in the past ten or twenty years was due to the weakness of the parties, or to the process of realignment, or to the particular politics of the time which reflected an alienation and distrust of all of the institutions of society, which is peculiar to the day and will lead to a new, more fragmented political system. The question is whether decline in partisanship and the recent (albeit stemmed in 1980) increase in ticket splitting by partisans is characteristic of the process of realignment, characteristic of a new alignment, or just an historic episode which is prelude to a new party system.

The Potential for Partisan Growth

The measure of decline in partisan identification does not point to the disappointment of the voter who has declared himself a Democrat or Republican in youth and then felt forced to desert the party. That happens, but the bulk of the decline is not in changed partisan attitudes as much as it is in the unformed partisan attachments of the young—the much publicized Baby Boom generation. It may be one of the ironies of the 1960s that one of the most politicized decades in this century fostered one of the least political generations. Many were turned off, a few were turned out, and the vast majority were very slow to begin voting. Levels of education have typically been a predictor of voting, but in this case, the education is higher and the voting is lower.

The catalcysms of the past few decades made many not want to think about politics, but there are less dramatic explanations available. The differences in lifestyle between this generation and its elders may be just as causal. Unlike their parents, the first order of business for today's young adult is not always to marry and begin a career. The young are far more unsettled, partly because of the economy, partly because the expectations are not the same.

If we know that voters develop partisan attachments as their life in the community takes on more meaning because they have children in need of education, or because they own property, it stands to reason that those who do not fit the mold will need to find other reasons for caring about who is elected to the town council or to the state legislature. There are indications that some of the patterns of the young may be reverting to the more traditional ways of life, but it is still not the same. The classic American family of a working husband supporting his wife and 2.5 children just no longer fits the majority of American households.

The Baby Boomers are the key to the future, particularly for those who measure the health of the political system by partisan attachment. William Schneider suggests that it is still too soon to be sure how they will settle their partisanship, but that by their own description, they are the most liberal age-group in the electorate.

Writing after the 1984 election, Schneider noted that while the young voted for Reagan by a margin of three-to-two, their reasons were varied, "all unrelated to ideology. Economic performance was one. So was the fact that Walter Mondale, with his 'old politics,' was not a very inspiring figure to young voters."[14] The most important reason most people (including the young) had for supporting the incumbent president was their positive evaluation of his performance in office.

Fifty-eight percent of the voters between eighteen and twenty-nine voted for the Republican candidate according to the *New York Times*/CBS exit poll.[15] Whether or not that means they will develop an attachment to the Republican party remains to be seen, but it is certainly an interesting first step. According to Schneider, ideology is one of the last things to change in a realignment, "if it changes at all," because the president must first demonstrate that his policies are effective. Only then do voters begin to accept his "vision of society."[16]

The changes that occur in aggregate partisanship are usually—not always—the result of the younger people coming into the process, rather than switching identification of older voters. In almost every way, the future is in their hands.

Another group apparently up for grabs are women, although the

Portrait of the Electorate (By Sex)

	The Vote in 1980			The Vote in 1984	
	Reagan (%)	Carter (%)	Anderson (%)	Reagan (%)	Mondale (%)
Men	55	36	7	61	37
Women	47	45	7	57	42
White men	59	32	7	68	31
White women	52	39	8	64	36
Black men	14	82	3	12	85
Black women	9	88	3	6	93
Men, 18–29	47	39	11	61	37
Women, 18–29	39	49	10	55	45
Men, 30–44	59	31	4	62	37
Women, 30–44	50	41	8	54	46
Men, 45–59	60	34	5	63	36
Women, 45–59	50	44	5	58	41
Men, 60 and older	56	40	3	62	37
Women, 60 and older	52	43	4	64	35
Married men		N.A.		65	34
Married women		N.A.		60	39
Unmarried men		N.A.		53	45
Unmarried women		N.A.		50	49
Republican men	87	8	3	94	5
Republican women	85	10	5	93	6
Democratic men	29	63	6	27	72
Democratic women	23	71	5	23	76
Independent men	60	27	10	67	31
Independent women	49	34	13	60	39

	The Vote in 1980			The Vote in 1984	
	Reagan (%)	Carter (%)	Anderson (%)	Reagan (%)	Mondale (%)
Men with less than high school education	51	47	2	54	46
Women with less than high school education	41	55	2	46	52
Male high school graduates	53	42	2	61	38
Female high school graduates	50	44	3	60	39
Men with some college	59	31	8	58	36
Women with some college	52	39	8	58	41
Men, college grads	58	28	11	65	34
Women, college grads	42	44	12	53	47
Men in the East	52	38	8	57	42
Women in the East	42	47	10	47	52
Men in the Midwest	55	37	6	63	35
Women in the Midwest	47	44	7	59	41
Men in the South	58	38	3	64	36
Women in the South	47	50	3	63	36
Men in the West	56	30	11	62	37
Women in the West	51	38	9	57	42

NOTE: From the *New York Times* / CBS News Poll, 4 November 1984, based on exit polling interviews.

results of the 1984 election, which many thought would be largely
determined by the "gender gap," does not entirely bear out the
hopes of feminists or the fears of others.

Historically, women not only voted less frequently than men,
they were also, if married, likely to vote the way their husbands
did. That situation is clearly changing. Women are now the largest
single segment in the voting age population (attributable partly to
the fact that they live longer and outnumber men), and they are
more apt to make their own decisions.

There is a gap between the way men and women voted in the last
two presidential elections. In both instances, substantially more
women voted Democratic than did men. In 1980, 9 percent more
women supported Carter, and in 1984, 5 percent more women
supported Mondale. The greatest gaps existed between men and
women in the East (10 percent), with women giving Mondale 52
percent of their vote: between men and women college graduates,
13 percent more women favored the Democrats; and between
younger men and women, there was an 8 percent difference between eighteen to twenty-nine year olds and 9 percent difference
between thirty to forty-four year olds.

If the 1984 election were closer, it is entirely possible women
would have made the difference. Although we do not have sufficient data at the moment to analyze other races, it may be that the
attention paid to the women's vote affected the outcome of other
elections. In Massachusetts, for instance, there was a relatively
wide margin between men and women in their support for John
Kerry, the Democratic nominee for the Senate over the Republican
nominee Ray Shamie.

The gap between men and women is based on differences about
aggression and social stability, rather than issues popularly associated with feminist causes. According to Alan Baron, the greatest gaps historically have been over the issues of prohibition and
gun control; the first putting women on the Republican right, the
second on the Democratic left. "But," according to Baron, "their
real position—for social stability—was the same."[17]

When the Republican party first led the battle for suffrage,
women were apt to vote for the GOP not only because it supported prohibition and isolationism after World War I, but also

because Republican women came from a higher social economic class than Democratic women and were, therefore, far more likely to vote.

In 1916, the last Presidential election before suffrage, the Democrats received 9.1 million votes; the Republicans, 8.5 million. In 1920, the Democratic vote was 9.1 million again; the GOP vote, 15.7 million. To be sure, all women did not vote Republican. Perhaps only 75%.[18]

Only two Republican presidential candidates have not done well with women: Barry Goldwater (who ran 2 percent more behind with women than men) and Ronald Reagan (who ran behind in 1980 and 1984). In the years between 1980 and 1984, the gap reached as high as 10 percent, largely attributed to distrust of Reagan's foreign policy on the one hand and Reagonomics on the other, which may perhaps be a reflection of the increased role of women in the market place, although that is not in itself a factor which would necessarily lead to a gap, even though women are in a weaker economic position than men.

According to Republican presidential campaign managers, the fortuitous downing of the Korean jet liner in 1983 and the president's tempered response to it helped Reagan's image among women considerably[19]—as did much of the advertising directed toward women by both the party beginning in 1983 and during the campaign in 1984. There are other explanations for the outcome of the 1984 election, as well as for the fact that 57 percent of the women who voted cast their ballots for Ronald Reagan. Doubtless, the most important one is that women—as men—made their decision on the basis of how they judged Reagan performed as president in his first term, and they made a favorable judgement.

According to a Harris poll published shortly after the 1984 presidential election, the gender gap gave the Democratic party a 57 to 43 percent female composition, and the Republican party a 52 to 48 percent female composition.[20] It is not just that women (who make up 53 percent of the population and tend to be older, hence their larger number in the parties) are moving to the Democrats; men are moving to the Republicans. According to Harris, evidence for this proposition is to be found among the independ-

ents, 57 percent of whom are male. If men are shifting their partisan identification, they would be apt to describe themselves as
independents before they make the final step to the other party.[21]

Of course no discussion of the women's vote would be complete
without mention of the vice-presidential candidacy of Representative Geraldine Ferraro in 1984. On the positive side, Ferraro's
candidacy unquestionably galvanized many volunteers around the
country, some of whom will undoubtedly stay active in politics.
Her greatest contribution may have been a broadening of the image
of a charismatic woman leader, a role not typically associated with
women in the United States. It was a bold and dramatic step
toward the inclusion of people, other than white males, at our
highest levels of government.

On the negative side, Republican pollsters found that 10 percent
of those who said they voted against Mondale (as opposed to voting
for Reagan) said they did so because of Mondale's choice of a
vice-presidential nominee. And for the first time in the experience
of at least one pollster, the vice-presidential nominees affected
between one and one and a half points in the election outcome.[22]

How much of the positive results and how much of the negative
results are due to the personality and events surrounding Geraldine
Ferraro particularly and how much to the fact that she is a woman
cannot be measured. Certainly, she was under far more scrutiny
from the press than any other vice-presidential nominee in history.
The fact that she was an Italian and an urban, Eastern liberal (not
a Southerner or someone perceived to be a more centrist Democrat
who might better "balance" the Democratic ticket) may have been
influential as well.

ELECTION PROCEDURES AND PARTY VOTING

One important reason for the decline in partisan identification
over the long haul has to do with changes within the American
voting population: levels of education; different (declined) incentives to join a party; less faith in the institutions, including the
parties, and so on. But the voter is not the only factor in the
equation. Changes in the procedures of elections have also had
their effect, acting to discourage straight party voting. In fact, most

analysts agree that American voter registration requirements are among the most restrictive in the world, putting the onus on the citizen rather than the state to insure registration in the first place. They also require varying periods of residence. Places and times to register are not easily accessible.

Perhaps the single greatest procedural reform to work against strong partisan identification was the adoption of the Australian ballot which lists all candidates for a particular office in one place and permits a voter to split his ticket. It is not that we are advocating a return to the party ballot, but merely noting that in the early years of this century, before the Australian ballot was widely adopted, a voter was given a party ballot and had no choice but to vote a straight party ticket. Given the public circumstances under which one would ask for a ballot and the tendency for voting to become a reinforcing habit, it is not surprising that voters were more partisan in earlier generations and were able to pass on their partisanship to their children.

Obviously, the reasons for the increase in ticket splitting in recent years are more complex, or at any rate more subtle, but the long view is distorted without a recognition of the coercive nature of party voting in the last century. By the end of the 1920s, ticket splitting reached a 20 percent high, declined during the Roosevelt years, and began climbing to a peak of about 45 percent in 1972 —at just that point when we believe the parties reached their nadir.[23] The analysis upon which these data are compiled compared the presidential vote to congressional district voting and does not, therefore, consider elections below the federal level, where, presumably, party voting is likely to be more uniform because of the lack of alternative information about the candidates.

Political scientists Warren Miller and Therese Levitan have suggested that one reason for the split at the presidential level has to do with the fact that the specific presidential candidates who have been nominated in recent years are not popular with sizable numbers of voters within their own party.[24] If Miller and Levitan are right (they certainly make a plausible argument with which few who have witnessed the presidential selection process over the last twenty years would argue) and looking at the span of ticket split-

ting with its decrease during the New Deal when the last realignment was absolutely known to have occurred, it seems clear that
voters are (and probably always have been) quite aware of making
partisan choices and willing to register disapproval. The proliferation of primaries and caucuses, which were initially designed to
weaken the capacity of party leaders to select candidates, are a
primary example of a reform that worked. It is now a subject of
much concern to many inside and outside politics, but it is a
problem endemic to a decentralized system.

Conclusion

There are a number of reasons given for the decline of partisan
identification in the United States since the middle of the century:
the decline of faith in the institutions; the rise of education and with
it the assumption that one is above parties; the mobility that makes
it more difficult for persons to establish the kinds of links normally
associated with partisan identifiers in a community; and so on. The
most important factor has been the appearance of a large, new
generation that came of age in an antiparty atmosphere. It is not
so much that the old partisans changed as it is that they faded away
and have been replaced in the statistical analyses by younger citizens who do not have the old attachments.

A theme we have reiterated throughout is that the weak party
system that existed into the beginning of the last decade was
created by the political reforms that went before. At a time of
change and at a time of conflict, the parties were not capable of
pressing for concensus or building a coalition. The pressures of the
times combine with the technology of the times, and opposing
views spread fast and wide. New voters and new ways of getting
a message across have had an impact on the parties.

According to a Gallup poll published December 1, 1984, those
who described themselves as being to the right of center increased
from 31 to 36 percent since 1976, while those who described themselves as being to the left of center decreased from 24 to 18 percent

in the same time period. Many would explain the shift to the right as a natural reaction to the movement to the left that characterized some important national policies in the 1960s. Another explanation is the personal success of a conservative president and, beyond him, of the New Right in getting its message across. A third is the inability of the more liberal Democratic party and its leaders to hold on to moderate followers, making the term "liberal" less attractive.

Fifty-six percent of the Republican party describes itself as conservative, making it a much more cohesive ideological grouping than Democrats, 27 percent of whom describe themselves as liberals, 38 percent as moderate, and 29 percent as conservative.[25] The labels of liberal and conservative have always been relative in American politics. Their popularity waxes and wanes with the ability of leaders to express their views and their vision of the world, and the effectiveness of government to implement those views in a way we can recognize as solving problems. Whether or not the labels continue to have significance for partisans will depend on both the politics and the parties.

The trend of declining partisanship has been stemmed in the last few years. Both parties have seen an increase in their party identifiers: Republicans increased from 26 to 34 percent in the year preceding the 1984 election, while Democrats increased from 41 to 42 percent—independents dropped from 28 to 20 percent.[26] Of course, the GOP had farther to go, suffering as it was from the ravages of Watergate on the one hand and its minority status since the New Deal realignment on the other. It has made an important comeback, and it may very well succeed in fostering a new alignment, taking in the South and West.

Whether or not it is appropriate to say the time of realignment is here, it is clear that the increase in Republican identifiers is due in large measure to the greater strength of the national Republican party, which has reached out to millions of households across the nation through the mail and reached even greater numbers (albeit less intensively) through paid media. The test will come at the end of the 1980s, when the party is no longer headed by the most popular American president since John Kennedy. It is then that the GOP may have to choose between the social issues that have motivated the New Right and the message of economic prosperity that has attracted the younger voters who tend to be liberal on social issues. It is the kind of debate more characteristically found in the heterogeneous Democratic party. It is the kind of debate likely to be found in a party seeking to represent more than a minority of the population.

It is our view that whether or not the Republican party succeeds in becoming the new majority party, or whether it succeeds in increasing its partisans to a third of the electorate, the measure of party strength in America should include more than the sense of identification voters are willing to make.

Belief in the parties is important to the stability of the system. Such faith sustains positive attitudes in a wide range of perceptions about ourselves as a society. It gives its adherents a position from which to view the world, to know what and whom to value. We would like to think that partisanship will continue to increase as the national parties continue to grow stronger. We do not think partisan identification is all there is when it comes to measuring party strength.

The measure we would like to apply to the strength of parties is voter behavior. We may be in transition from one political alignment to another; certainly political observers have been writing about the realigning process for some time. But the balance we have today may be the balance we get, which is to say that slightly more than one-third of the population will identify itself as Democratic, one-third as Republican, and slightly less than one-third as independents. Among the independents, most will lean toward one or the other of the two major parties. They will make their decisions partly on the basis of long-held beliefs and partly on their assessments of what each party has to offer in any given election. They will judge presidential races on the performance of the incumbent when there is one or on the promises of a new candidate and his or her party and their assessment of his or her ability to fulfill those promises. They will make their choice for congressional office based on what they know about the candidates (an ever-increasing amount of information), and how they judge the behavior of the party in power in the White House.

Thus far, incumbency matters more than anything else when it comes to voter behavior in most elections. Usually, this is because we know more about incumbents than we know about challengers. The possibility of change in voter behavior may come when challengers have the ability to get out more information about their candidacy. We believe that ability will depend increasingly upon the role of the parties as the single most important player, outside of the campaign, in electoral politics.

PART
IV

CONCLUSION

7

The New Party System

WHAT WE HAVE DESCRIBED in the previous chapters
is a centralized, national party organization, where power and
resources flow from the top down. A structure exists in Washington and at the state level, but the volunteers and political hacks,
who were not qualified for appointment to office, who used to
populate it at all levels, have been replaced by professionals. There
remains a place for volunteers and there remains a role for the
party membership at large, but it is a different one than most
political observers thought it was.

Today's political party is stronger, not only because it is more
professional and has more money, but because it is now in a relatively better position to influence the outcomes of elections and the
behavior of government than it was before, and more than any
other single actor on the political scene. The campaign finance law
was designed to limit the undue influence of special interests and,
in the process, it has left the parties in a healthier position vis-a-vis
those interests. The law has encouraged greater reliance by candidates on the parties, and the parties have moved dramatically into

the role of providing campaign services that gives it an increasing role in the selection of its nominees.

The emergence of strong, national, professional parties comes after a half century of party reform which weakened the structure to the point that by the latter half of this century, the organizational structure was barely alive, although much of the population still held onto a kind of residual party loyalty. All that was left to sustain the parties was the labeling of candidates in elections and the organizing of legislatures. As we moved toward the last quarter of the century, partisan identification slid because new generations of citizens had grown up and the parties failed to capture their loyalty. Independence became a positive virtue. Although close analysis suggests that a large portion of the independent vote tends to lean toward one party or the other, and that "leaners" are apt to be as predictable in their voting behavior as partisan voters, they are nonetheless a standing testament to the weakness of the party system.

Whether or not the parties succeed in gaining the loyalty of the next generations will depend on what they have to offer. That, after all, is the crux of the issue for the future. Loyalty is something to be earned, and the ability of the parties to win that loyalty will depend almost entirely on what kinds of candidates they can put up and what principles they stand upon. Our measure of party strength includes control of nominations, the ability to raise and sustain party resources in the face of competition from other groups, and the capacity of the party to influence government. Strong support from the voters should follow an effective resolution of these factors, but certainly cannot be expected to precede them.

Building the New Party System

By the time the parties were completely "reformed" and had lost the major part of their power, it became apparent that they had little to offer the voters and little capacity to handle the social and political pressures that were mounting in the United States in the latter part of the 1960s. Although it was clear that something was needed to improve their position in the political world, it was not clear they would succeed and the prognosis was dim indeed.

David Broder concluded *The Party's Over* with a recounting of the despair so many felt in this last quarter of the twentieth century.

> Above all, I have heard the conversations of hundreds of average Americans, who see their world, their plans, their hopes crumbling, and do not know where to turn. I cannot forget the doctor's widow in Richmond, Virginia, who said, "You can't tell from day to day, but if it doesn't do better than it is now, it won't be much of a country. This is the saddest situation I've ever seen. I've seen this country go through four wars and a depression and this is the worst." I remember all too well the young husband in New Rochelle, New York, with his arm around his wife's shoulders, who told a visitor of the fears for the future that have caused them to delay starting a family. "We've even thought seriously of moving to some other country," he said, "but we don't know where to go."[1]

It is still painful to recall the lack of hope, and the cynicism we learned to adopt when thinking about the country and ourselves. To Broder, the answer lay only in our own hands, and the best solution lay with the parties: We needed first of all to strengthen the machinery of the parties and government. We needed also to strengthen the relationship between the presidency and Congress; to expand the role of party caucuses and party leaders in Congress; to reduce the number of elected officials in state government in order to strengthen the governors and state legislatures; to reduce the elected officials at the local level and encourage two-party competition; to strengthen the presidential nominating procedure, making the parties more responsible; to discipline the use of money in politics; and to strengthen the party organizations and their staffs so that they could recapture the campaign management functions.[2]

Much of what Broder called for, we have tried to change. Moving at the lugubrious pace of a loosely flung together institution, we have changed our body politic. We have altered our laws and have tried on new goals and new self-images. We have dramatically changed the parties—the first and final step of David Broder's charge.

The two major parties responded characteristically to the challenge: the Democrats sought to improve their processes by extending the franchise of active party participation to those who had been left out (women, minorities, and youth); the Republicans (always a more homogeneous party and less inclined to organize in terms of their separate constituencies) focused on their organizational strength, making a committed effort toward fund raising and professionalism. One party learned from the other, and the GOP broadened its group of active participants while the Democrats began to employ the techniques used by their opponents.

Both parties became more ideologically coherent, with more conservative Democrats voting Republican and liberal Republicans finding themselves more at home with the Democrats. This cleaning up of the middle was not a complete job, however, and many Americans found themselves somewhat remote from their party leaders and the candidates the party put forth in nomination for a time. Still, extremists in both parties have had to compromise, and there does seem to be less likelihood today that either the Far Right or the Far Left will capture control. Regional differences also remain, supported in part by the structure of state and the federal legislatures, which discourage legislators from switching their party allegiance lest they lose seniority.

CONTROL OF NOMINATIONS

In 1976, the Republican National Committee began intervening in state primaries to find the best candidate possible to run against the Democrats in the general election. Although the party is restricted by law and treated like a nonparty organization in primary elections (for example, limited to a $5,000 contribution), the legitimacy of party endorsement is certainly a strategic advantage in an election that draws mostly the party faithful.

Perhaps the most important factor leading to party intervention was the party's candidate recruitment program. If the party were to encourage strong, qualified people to run for office, especially when the party was in the minority, it would have to make some promises of support. The assistance of the party during the election, by providing funds, legal advice, accounting aids, and a multiplicity of other campaign services, could be critical to the success of a candidate who had never run for office before. The Democrats, too, have begun recruiting candidates and offering support.

Another element leading to the control of its candidates was the more subtle use of party resources to train and guide candidates and campaign workers in party practices and in the acceptance of party positions on a very wide range of issues. It was not that candidates for office lacked views of their own, but rather that most campaigns tend to be about one or two issues, and many individuals entered elective politics after participation in a single issue. Now the candidate can be "briefed" on a spectrum of issues, and because much of the briefing material is provided by the party, the influence of party philosophy may be tremendous.

How much influence the party will have in controlling the behavior of incumbent office holders remains to be seen, but the 1981 effort by the RNC to encourage voters to write their representatives in support of the president's tax program was impressive. The House and Senate campaign committees usually carry more weight than the national committees in both parties. And as their importance to candidates grows, their importance in the party proper grows. Partisan voting in Congress has increased in the last few years and that is perhaps the best measure of the party's ability in influencing public policy.

PARTY RESOURCES

Despite the predictions by many that the campaign finance law would seriously hurt the parties, a positive outcome of the law may turn out to be the advantage the parties have over the interests in raising and, particularly, in spending money.

One part of that advantage is the greater amount individuals can contribute to the parties relative to either candidates or political action committees ($1,000 to the former and $5,000 to the latter, compared to $20,000 to the party). There are also large loopholes in the law that make party contributions effectively unlimited because the federal law speaks only to federal elections. The parties, in other words, are one of the few last bastions of fat cats.

Another advantage that parties have over other groups is their greater legitimacy in the long run. They are not new, unknown organizations which spring up with each election or each political crisis. They can appeal to supporters on long-standing issues, or they can appeal to supporters on the politics of the moment: gaining or keeping control of the legislature; specific issues without standing constituencies such as supporting or opposing particular public figures. (The departure of James Watt, while a boon to the environment, was definitely costly to both national parties and probably to the environmental groups as well because of the allure of his name on direct mail appeals and fund raising events for both supporters and opponents.)

The advantage of legitimacy was more pronounced in the controversial years just past when some of the big independent spending groups on the New Right were charged with raising millions of dollars and spending relatively little of it. As independent spending becomes more popular, the parties may also become more important vehicles for participation by the small donors who may become skeptical of unknown groups that spring up and ask for donations for every dramatic cause. Not knowing who is legitimate and who is not may lead some people to prefer the party that is known over the interest group that is not.

Because the presidential campaign is publicly financed, and the conditions of accepting public funds require the campaigns to forego private contributions, both large and small donors are left only with the parties if they want to participate. Experience has shown that many Americans are motivated by the importance of the presidential election and the media attention it gets to do just that: to exercise their civic responsibility by contributing their money, if not their time and energy, as a measure of commitment to the candidate, the party, or just to the process itself.

Another consequence of the law is that it encourages the organizers of presidential campaigns to centralize their activities as much as possible in order to avoid spending too much in one place. Most, if not all, of the local tasks must be turned over to the state party to fulfill, and even though relations between the party and the national campaign are invariably strained, the law has encouraged greater participation by the party and greater dependence on the party by the campaign. It may take several such elections to build an amicable relationship, but both parties are actively working to improve the situation.

INFLUENCING PUBLIC POLICY

We described two ways the GOP has acted to influence policy: it prepared briefing material on issues for candidates during the campaign period, which had the effect of defining the positions of many candidates on a wide range of issues, and it has conducted media and direct campaigns to party members and the public at large to urge constituents to write their congressmen supporting administration programs.

Other instances of party influence have also been seen in the last few years, including the denial of party perks to Democratic members who consistently vote against their party in the House. When Phil Gramm from Texas was stripped of his seat on the House budget committee because he did not support the party, he switched parties and ran for re-election as a Republican. His case was unusual because it showed the extremes to which both the party and the incumbent were willing to go to express principles. It was, however, within the general direction of party influence and congressional adherence. (Gramm, by the way, won re-election to the House, and in 1984, won election to the Senate as a Republican from Texas.)

Party leadership has always been relatively respectful of regional differences within the party and allowed a member of Congress a certain amount of freedom in taking positions on issues, particularly if that issue was relevant to re-election. The Gramm case suggests that the freedom is declining and congressional party leadership on both sides of the aisle expect more loyalty.

The other major attempt by parties to influence office holders outside of legislatures (which are organized around parties) has been the platform drawn up for the national presidential nominating convention. Michael Malbin made a strong case for the proposition that the platform is a party creature and does matter when it comes to evaluating the effectiveness of a president in office.[3] The platform is the most important opportunity party membership and leadership have to come together and address the issues of the day and the principles upon which the party will stand. The popular prejudice sees the writing of the platform as an idle exercise. We think it is time we disavow that view and recognize the role of the party apparatus in defining the issues, its importance as a symbol of what the party stands for, and the political consequences of its impact on elections and especially on administrations that are judged by them.

The Party of the Future

In many respects, the party of the future is here; it is the gap in perception of this fact that binds us to the past. If a new animal is lurking in the guise of a dead system, it will emerge sooner or later, and there may not be anything to be done about it at all. We think it is important to know what has happened and to consider the possibilities for the future, partly because it is our system of government and something we must responsibly cherish, and partly because we still seem intent on "ironing out the wrinkles" in the political system. The spirit of reform has not entirely died. The potential for leadership to improve upon or undermine growth always exists.

VOLUNTEERS IN THE NEW PARTY SYSTEM

The political elite—the tiny percentage of the population that actively participates in electoral politics—used to organize campaigns, and fill the posts of party office from election district captains to party chairpersons. Committee membership led from precinct, to ward, to city, county, state, and national levels. There were other committees as well on rules, issues, and so on. There were honorary groups within the parties for large donors who could gain access to high elected officials and special perks at party conventions in return for their contributions. The honorary groups did not necessarily give anything more than money to the party, but they did make their power felt as they sought to influence public policy.

Many of these players remain in the new party. From the 1960s they dominated all givers in the Democratic party and were few and far between in the GOP after Watergate. Today both parties rely on small donors for more than 60 percent of their income, but the large donors are still invited to special meetings and still feel free to call upon party leaders to press their interests and arrange for private get-togethers with those in office. Power attracts them, and there is, if anything, more rather than less power in today's party.

The political hacks, whether paid or unpaid, still hang about, but their role is severely curtailed. There used to be what might be referred to as "The Savior of the Week" syndrome, wherein every campaign could rely on someone dropping by the headquarters, willing to tell the staff just what was required to turn the campaign around because he or she was "in touch with The People" (having talked to a cab driver on the way over). If the Savior was sufficiently esteemed by the staff and willing to take a hand in trying out the new tactic, it might be added to the repertoire. More typically, the staff would try to ignore the interruption and continue the battle of sorting out the power structure within the campaign organization. Polling has helped to eliminate much of the uncertainty about what people are thinking and what is likely to motivate them to vote.

Today, campaigns are run by professionals (and even volunteers) who are trained in their tasks and who rely on advice and assistance from the national and state parties and the private consulting firms they employ to do their advertising, fund raising, and general campaigning. There is less room for ad hoc campaign strategy and there are definite restraints on unplanned expenditures. Storefronts may still exist, but they are not the seat of campaign decision making. In fact, they tend to do very little at all but pass out literature or house phone banks. And even the phone banks tend to be run by professional callers who can be trained and relied upon to complete their assigned tasks.

Case work was another function of local parties in the days of yore. When people needed help in coping with the public (or even private) authorities, they could turn to the party to mediate on their behalf. As local parties become less visible, that function has fallen more and more to elected officials who typically hire a staff of one or two to provide that service. Little city halls and local congressional offices are recent phenomena and represent the shift of functions.

What then is left for the new volunteer, and how will the party continue to perform that integrating function of linking private citizens with public roles and responsibilities? The parties may not have generated much activism in the past several decades, but issues, and in some cases, candidates have certainly motivated people. Gary Hart's largely volunteer campaign organization in New Hampshire reached 80,000 households in the cold primary season in 1984; Walter Mondale's organization reached over 90,000 in New Hampshire. The Reagan campaign claims to have gotten 600,000 volunteers out during the general election nationwide.[4]

Finding volunteers for voter registration, canvassing, and getting out the vote remain a vehicle for participation, although it is not as essential as it once was. Campaigns used to be far more labor-intensive operations, but that is no longer the case. Bodies can still be used to stand on busy intersections holding signs during rush hour, but many of the traditional tasks have been taken over by machines or by professionals in today's more centralized campaign organizations.

One critical question the parties and their campaign organizations must resolve is how to motivate support, and once motivated, how to apply it in a meaningful way for both the participant and the organization. It goes back to the question of incentives and rewards, which is the basis of all organizations. It goes back to the constant theme of would-be party leaders that they want to "rebuild the grassroots."

It is our contention that the part of motivation dependent upon communication—upon reaching the minds (and maybe hearts) of party supporters—is very much within the sphere of party control. If anything, it has improved in quality and in quantity. Some of that communication has been in the form of direct mail solicitations which provide the recipient the opportunity to act on it, and as many fund raisers know, commitment tends to follow money: once you invest money in a cause, you come to believe in it more strongly. In that regard, then, it is likely that millions of Americans have a more firmly rooted commitment to their party.

But what of those who want to come out and contribute their spare time and energy? One reality everyone must face (including those who would like to contribute their time) is that there is less of it around these days. Seventy percent of the women under thirty-five work. Both women and men want to spend more time with their families and more time in health-related activities. The question is What can an organization do with individuals who want to make a contribution but have limited time and, usually, little to offer beyond their enthusiasm?

There will undoubtedly be many efforts made by both parties to find satisfying useful tasks. The probability remains, however, that the only elections to rely entirely on that sort of grassroots efforts will be local elections. Even state legislative races have become more expensive and more dependent on the sophisticated campaign technologies available, as PAC money moves increasingly in that direction.

Politics appears to be becoming a more passive activity, but it should be borne in mind that the percentage of the population who used to be active was always small and not always representative of the population as a whole. The legitimacy and acceptance of the entire system depended and continues to depend not on this small elite but on the proportion of the population who vote. They are being reached; they are better informed; they may be more committed in the future. More of them are contributing money to the parties, and they may feel that their participation is anything but passive, given that it was more than they did before, and they are engaged in more communication with the party as a result of their donation.

CANDIDATES IN THE NEW PARTY SYSTEM

If the party has better control over the nomination, then clearly there should be some discernible difference between the candidates for office under the new and old systems. The greatest influence thus far has been seen in candidates for Congress: they are the ones most dependent on the national party committees; they are of less interest to state and local parties; they are more subject to the special interest groups, especially those based in Washington.

At the risk of generalization, we would characterize the candidates of a few years ago as more likely to have been self-selected. They were apt to have a good media image. They may or may not have been backed by important interests in the constituency or important factions of the party. In recent years, under the new campaign reform legislation, they have tended to be relatively wealthy and free to spend as much of their own money as they chose, as the law exempts from limitation what a candidate puts into his own race. Because of their independence, they mounted their own organizations and spent a good deal of time and energy maintaining them once in office.

The self-selected candidate voted with leadership on the important question of organizing the House or Senate, but he was more independent on almost every other question. The class of 1974 was particularly notable for its rebellion against the seniority system, which reflected the impatience of these freshmen legislators to demonstrate their strength and worth to their constituents and the nation at large.

The independence exhibited by the old candidates is less likely to characterize the new candidates. Allowances will still be made for constituent variations, but the party is less apt to tolerate much prima donna behavior because the candidate will truly be less independent. If the party recruits and trains candidates and provides the backbone of their campaigns, they are likely to end up as a more homogeneous group and more inclined to be team players. It is not likely that the party will ever completely dominate candidate selection because there are differences among regions and, perhaps more importantly, those who seek office tend to be people of strong ambition who are interested in power.

The national party will also be apt to involve itself more and more in gubernatorial and state legislative races partly because of its interest in reapportionment, and partly because these offices are often the first step up the ladder and places to groom prospective national leaders.

THE PRESIDENCY

The one area the party appears now to have least influence over is the presidential nomination. The main obstacle to party control over this obviously important office is the number of primaries that determine the vote of so many delegates to the nominating conventions. Recent Democratic reforms that provide for a significant portion of uncommitted delegates go some length toward overcoming the primary problem, but they are, as yet, insufficient.

The primaries are not, however, the only impediment to party control over the presidential nomination. The singular importance of the presidency combines with the media focus to limit the influence of the party. Except for the fact that those who could reasonably aspire to the office would usually come up through the party ranks, and therefore be influenced by it, the office is relatively independent. On the other hand, the influence of the party is quite strong on the presidency when it comes to the party platform, as already noted. Delegates negotiate important points, but the bulk of the program comes from the party, and the measure of the president's first year in office is usually based on his implementation of the platform.

Beyond setting the presidential agenda, the other major party role has been in appointments to office. Although the point has been made that there have been recent incursions into that province of the party by issue networks, it has always remained true that most appointees to office must pass party muster. A cabinet secretary may now require more expertise and support from constituent interest groups of that department than used to be the case, but he or she must also be acceptable to the party because of past identification and work, or because the prospective appointee would reflect well on the party. As a representative of the administration, appointees are expected to support party candidates.

The interesting question remains of what impact this relative independence has on the political system. One of the strongest arguments in favor of parties has been that they are a kind of mortar that holds the American system together, enabling us to overcome the separation of powers built into the constitution. Unlike a parliamentary system, electing a president does not necessarily mean support in Congress because the parties may divide the branches of government, or because the president is a weak leader of his party.

One's position on this question may depend on one's view of government. If you believe in strong government, then a bridging of the separation of powers is important because there is little built into the structure to encourage action. If you believe in less government, then the checks and balances work for you. In those few instances in American history when the mortar held, the president enjoyed overwhelming support in Congress: the period of reconstruction; the depression years; and the early years of the Johnson administration when he tried to build the Great Society. In each case the members of Congress owed their seats to the coattails of the president.

We are posing a different situation: a circumstance where the members of Congress owe their seats to the support of the national party rather than the personal strength of the president (or, as is often the case, the personal weakness of the opposing party's candidate). A number of Republicans (for example Bob Kasten, Wisc.; Mark Mattingly, Ga.; Jeremiah Denton, Ala.; Don Nichols, Okla.; Alfonse D'Amato, N.Y.; and John East, N.C.) won their seats in the Senate in 1980 with a combination of help from the Reagan momentum on the one hand, and the massive amount of money made available to them by the National Republican Senatorial Campaign, which ranged from $500,000 to $1 million. It comes down to a question of allegiance and the relationship that exists between the party and the president. How powerful would either side have to be? Is it likely that there would be a serious conflict?

Prediction is chancy. Our guess, however, is that accommodation would be more likely than war between a president and his party. If there is a strong party—one that remains relatively independent of the White House because it has resources and because of the role it plays in the election of so many officials at all levels of government—the party will be primarily interested in maintaining its strength in winning election. It will not recklessly oppose its president because he can always take his case to the voters. Nor, we believe, will a president recklessly oppose his party given his dependence on the party's role in getting out the vote and in supporting those needed to pass legislation in Congress.

WINNING VERSUS IDEOLOGY

One perennial topic of discussion among party theorists concerns the question of ideological purity, or, put another way, whether or not they are responsible institutions: if you vote for a candidate for the presidency because of his platform, is he able to implement it, or is he caught up by the checks and balances between the branches on the one hand and the need for accommodation within his party on the other hand?

In the 1950s, the American Political Science Association issued a report calling for a more responsible party system, but since then, the idea has fallen into disrepute. Serious political practitioners accused the thinkers of being fuzzy. Serious political scientists tended to take the same view, considering themselves and the parties as more pragmatic than that. What was important—what sustained the party—was winning office.

Not wanting to risk being considered frivolous, we, too, agree that winning office is what sustains the party. But it has also become clear in recent years that winning office requires some commitment to principles, and that one of the characteristics of party weakness in the past has been that they "don't mean a dime's worth of difference." The question is how much commitment, at what risk to the capacity to compromise?

There is no clear line to be drawn between rigidity and flexibility, between what is possible to compromise and what is too far beyond our imagination to accept as plausible. The pressure to increase ideological coherence, to become more principled, does not come from the party's center, it always comes from the outsiders. When the outsiders become part of the inner circle, they are captured by the view from the top and usually moderate their views, or at the very least, their strategies. It is an almost inevitable process that is seen in every sort of organization. "Where you stand depends on where you sit," is one description. Organization theorists sometimes speak of "suboptimization," which views the process from the other end: those lower down in the organization do not see the whole picture and press for the success and advancement of their department over others. Although we are concerned with several organizations, the process is not dissimilar.

In the midst of George McGovern's campaign for the presidency in 1972, Gary Hart, then his campaign manager, said at a staff meeting that anyone on the staff who did not put George McGovern before any interest or any group did not belong in the campaign. The McGovern campaign was as much made up of interest groups as any campaign in recent years, and there was general agreement that Hart was right. Those who came to the staff because of their role in feminist organizations or Vietnam Vets against the War were forced to switch their sense of allegiance, not because Hart said so, but because of the change in their perspectives from advocate to a representative of the established power, the Democratic party in this instance. It was a process involving some ambivalance. It undoubtedly touched each individual's sense of ambition as well as honor. But it always happened and, we would judge, it always will because the power at stake accedes that of any single group or interest.

People may, and often do, start out in public life as issue advocates. The closer they get to the top, the nearer they get to core of electoral politics, the more they become politicians: people who want to be part of the process and who use issues as chips that they move around as part of their bid to be included in the game. We do not mean to suggest that politicians do not hold genuine beliefs about the issues or more general philosophies of how government ought to function. Most do, and most believe strongly in the proposition that their participation will make a difference to the happiness of humanity. But the need to be involved, to be part of the process is not inconsistent with the need to make life better. Those who participate in political life from one year to the next know that each campaign brings different questions to be decided in that never-ending struggle toward the greater happiness.

The question we might ask ourselves is what happens when the issues are derived from a moral and religious background? Is it a struggle between temporal and eternal power in which the political party—indeed the entire political process—is lower down on the organizational scale when put in relation to The Eternal? In that case, the process of adaptation to the give and take of politics would not happen; the desire to be part of the process is not strong enough to counter the sure knowledge of what is right and what is wrong. The willingness to compromise would all but disappear and should individuals so motivated come to dominate the parties, the capacity of the system to attain consensus would also disappear.

The fear of such a party take over underlies the thoughts of political analysts when they speak of the parties becoming dominated by the interests, becoming ideological. It is not that we think the fear is unreasonable, but rather that we believe it to be improbable. Although we suspect the public would be surprised at the number of genuinely religious people who participate in politics, we do not think that the sort of person who is driven by such a clear and certain light tends to stay in politics very long, or tends to rise very far in the inner circles. An individual may succeed from time to time (perhaps especially in these times), but the emergence of such a number of them as to oust the more traditional political personality is not likely.

If we can put that fear behind us then, the question still stands of how much principle is enough to give coherence and meaning to the parties? The answer must be enough to offer a sensible choice, a program for action that would be different, but not revolutionary. The differences between the parties must be sufficient to be perceived by the voters who can feel that there is a choice to be made. That knowledge is dependent both on the programs of the parties and their ability to communicate the differences.

COMMUNICATION AND THE NEW PARTY SYSTEM

By the end of the 1980s, both parties will probably have their own cable networks reaching out to the party faithful, educating them to the party's principles and the skills required for running campaigns. The lists of registered voters maintained by the parties and their affiliates will be more extensive, and the communication between the party and the voters will increase accordingly in the mails, by telephone, probably even by computer. More people will have access to more information than ever before and that, we believe, will lead to an increase in partisan intensity. The capacity to communicate so much so easily will make our politics much less labor-intensive, not unlike many of the activities in the rest of our lives.

The increased communication may mean that politics becomes more passive because so much of the former activity had to do with reaching out to voters. Certainly many of the old tasks are no longer relevant, and the campaign finance law has added to the passivity by requiring a centralization of the process in order to keep track of the income and expenditures. The general election of the president makes that point most dramatically because it is the one most likely to generate the greatest amount of enthusiasm. But the public financing prohibits contributions directly to the campaigns, and the spending limitations (combined with the uncertain relations between the presidential campaign staff and state and local parties) encourage even more centralization. It is a time when many people want to do more and find that there is less to do. The fact that there is less for the volunteer to do and the fact that, presidential elections aside, there are fewer volunteers is both cause and effect of the new circumstances.

Someday, someone may solve the problem of what to do with volunteers in a way that is both satisfying to the volunteer and productive to the party and the campaign. Organizations must find a way of making themselves efficient if they are to survive, and it is not likely that irrelevant work, or unsatisfying participation, will sustain anything for very long, even if campaigns are temporary phenomena. It is likely that the solution will have less to do with communication and more with other organizational tasks, such as decision making, unless we begin training more individuals in the technology of tomorrow's communication systems—not an unlikely prospect.

The professionalization of politics has its strengths and its weaknesses. It is part and parcel of the new system, however, and it brings us back to the focus of this book. We have been writing principally about the people who actively participate: the party structure and the individuals who make it work. It has been our view that the parties lost ground with the voters because they did not mean very much. One reason they lost control of their destiny was because most of the reforms in this century effectively weakened the structure—the ability of party leaders to make their organizations do very much at all. The strength of the new party system rests on the capability of these new professionals to make decisions about candidates and issues, and to reach out to the citizenry and make those decisions known.

PARTY LEADERSHIP

In some respects the parties seem like giant amoeba covering the political environment. Everything falls under them, but they are formless. Political observers talk about party decline, or even party resurgence, but the parties seem to shift only slightly, shuddering perhaps in the South as realignment takes place. They are hard to grasp intellectually; they are certainly not easy to grasp in the day-to-day practice of politics by political leaders. If parties are about power, then those who participate in them want power and they are loathe to give it away to someone else. What is required of party leadership is a reshifting of the power structure to emphasize some things and move away from others. It is one reason the parties move slowly: it is not an organization with easy measures for success or failure. Elections can be won and lost for so many reasons, most of them having to do with the personalities of the candidates and the specific choices voters make between candidates.

Many people working together—sometimes working at odds with each other—have brought about dramatic changes in both major parties in the last few years. The effort seems herculean when viewed in retrospect, but it inched along with many seeming backward steps at the time. Even with all of that effort, to most observers and to most voters, the parties seem to be not very different. They still appear to be as inefficient and amoebalike as ever. Part of leadership is bringing about change, and part of it is raising our expectations. We would argue that things have changed; we are only awaiting someone to point that out and lift our spirits about what can be.

This is not to say that we have not had political leadership during this time, but rather to suggest that the leaders we have had brought new generations into the parties and that it is to those new participants we must look for evidence of the style and substance of the changes that are taking place.

In the Republican party, the battle raged along class and regional lines as much as ideology. In the Democratic party, it was generational more than anything, but the new generation grew up in a markedly different environment and held very different values than its predecessors. Republican changes were first seen with the nomination of Barry Goldwater; the Democratic candidacies of Robert Kennedy and later George McGovern reflected the beginning of a shift within the Democratic party (most of the young people brought into the process by Eugene McCarthy did not remain past the 1968 campaign).

There are similarities between the new activists in both parties: They are more professional; they think of themselves as being more pragmatic; they tend to be more inclusive in their decision-making style than exclusive or elitist. They are concerned about the organizational structure of the parties and they have paid attention to rebuilding. David Broder, with whose observations about the need for party rebuilding we began this book, described the new participants in *The Changing of the Guard,* published in 1980. Both he and Xandra Kayden, writing in 1974, characterized the new people as "organizers."[5] Broder said of them "The next ones who will take power—the babies born between 1930 and 1955—were shaped in a very different time. Theirs has been a time of affluence and inflation, of extraordinary educational advance, and of wrenching social change and domestic discord."[6] Their objective is to change the system, not to destroy it. Their style is cool, in keeping with a television age. They contrast themselves with earlier generations who were either less educated or more elitist, and with the radicals of their own years who lost faith with the society.

This new generation, which itself will be replaced someday, has a quiet technocratic quality to it. If it were not that the individuals involved were forged out of the turmoil of the 1960s and 70s, they might seem rather boring. They can and have transformed the party structure, but they have yet to transform the public mind. It might be that we need to await another kind of personality with the capacity to mold the imagination as well as the organization.

That sort of leadership rarely addresses itself to structure, but then there is not so much need as there used to be. The organization is there, it is capable of being the platform for another step in another direction.

It is our view that the voters will not become strong partisans until imaginative leadership binds their hopes to the structure. The intensity of today's politics of morality and frustration may be part of that process, but we would hope for something more positive in the long run. We would hope that tolerance and a generosity of spirit enter the equation lest the partisanship become not a vehicle for structuring political thought but the front lines of battle.

The parties go on partly because the political system depends on them, even if the citizenry feels their inadequacy from time to time. They go on despite our rather feckless attitude toward them. It is our view that the parties have responded to the caring attention that those who love them have bestowed and have emerged in the 1980s as strong institutions capable of recapturing their innate functions, capable of having meaning to the voters. We expect that partisanship will increase in the 1990s if nothing cataclysmic interferes to alter our political structure.

The parties have changed because the old structures no longer worked and a new generation fought for and won the mantle of leadership. The new organization reflects the values of those leaders and the circumstances of today's society: incredibly rapid and intense communication; varied, private lifestyles; a certain cynicism or caution about all our institutions and the people who lead them. The changed expectations about women may turn out to be one of the most profound.

IS THERE A TWO-PARTY BALANCE: CAN THE DEMOCRATS CATCH UP?

It is our view that the party of the future is just about here and many would agree that the recently-found strength of the Republican party is not only a new phenomenon but an awesome power. Its strength is based on fund raising, which has netted the GOP approximately three times what comes into Democratic coffers. It uses the money to provide the latest technology and the best services it can to its candidates. It also uses it in the old political ways such as paying for travel of campaigners (which is how more than half of the Senate Republicans made their way to North Carolina to support Jesse Helms' battle against James Hunt in the most expensive Senate race in 1984, with $25 million raised).[7]

The concern of many is not whether the Republican party is the party of the future, but whether the Democrats can survive and compete in a reasonable balance against the Republicans. There are several points to be made about Democratic competitiveness.

The first is to point out that campaigns are apt to be competitive because of the tendency of the "out" party to gain strength as the "in" party makes mistakes. If one side has a major monetary advantage, the other uses it in its call for support from those who would oppose the interests of the first side. It may not work out evenly (Hunt raised only $9.15 million compared to the Helms take of $15.98 million), but it was not an insignificant amount.[8] The same argument can be made about the balance between the parties proper, although it takes far longer to even itself out because the sense of urgency campaign fund raisers use is rarely available to the parties as permanent institutions.

The balance in election funds holds for almost every election, with the exception of the presidential race. Independent spending by conservative groups favoring the GOP substantially outweighs the spending by liberal groups favoring the Democrats although labor's contribution in money and other resources balances the New Right. On the other hand, it remains to be seen whether or not such spending makes a difference in an election of wide visibility. So far, at least, it has not appeared to have been critical.

A second argument about party balance is that the financial advantage of the Republican party has always been offset by the interests allied with the Democratic party, which frequently assume tasks for the Democrats that the GOP undertakes on its own, such as voter registration and get-out-the-vote efforts. Although we believe the Democratic dependence on these groups has retarded the party's development, we think the circumstances are sufficiently changed to encourage the Democrats to develop capacities similar to the Republicans, relying less on the interests who have been somewhat constrained by the campaign finance laws. During

Manatt's tenure as party chairperson, the Democrats went from a 12:1 to a 3:1 ratio of fund raising compared to Republicans.

Another factor which traditionally offsets the GOP advantage is that Democratic donors tend to make their political contributions to the candidates rather than the parties. Only occasionally do Republican campaigns outspend Democratic campaigns and that, after all, is one of the most important tests of party parity. The giving pattern is due, in some measure at least, to the fact that Democrats are more likely to be incumbents. As incumbents Democratic candidates have existing organizations to solicit funds, maintain records, and offer the kinds of returns in influence that many donors like to think they are getting for their contribution.

The combined activity of the allied interest groups (most notably organized labor), and the giving pattern to campaigns rather than the party, accounts for much of the disparity between the Republicans and Democrats, but it does not completely even the score. It does not obviate the need for the Democrats to emulate the Republican fund raising activities, particularly if those who organize the balance sheets include the independent spending of the New Right groups, which were created, in part, to offset labor's influence.

The third argument about party balance is based on what might be called "historical inevitability" (which we cited in chapter 3 on party resurgence). A two-party system has always balanced itself out. If the organization is strong in one party, it will be strong in the other, as in Indiana which has one of the strongest two-party systems in the states. If the party organization is weak, the other side will also be weak. If one party dominates, it will function in factions and the other side will operate as another faction as has been characteristic of Southern politics.

The professionalization of the political parties at the national level is typically led by the Republicans who, according to Cornelius Cotter and John Bibby, are always the first to make changes, followed by the Democrats after an eight to twelve year lag, depending on when they lost the presidency.[9] The new Democratic headquarters building is almost symbolic of the new sense of institutionalism and professionalism in the Democratic party.

Looking back, with all of the advantages of hindsight, it is clear that the parties reached their nadir in the early 1970s. The Republicans, believing themselves to be in danger of slipping even further behind (down at times to 19 percent in the polls), if not facing absolute extinction, had to do something to dramatically alter their circumstances. It was the sort of organizational crisis that many organizations face and either fail or use as an opportunity to develop new methods of survival in recognition of the changed environment in which they live.

The Democrats watched, but not too closely because they were back in power. It was only when the resources and skills of the new Republican party began to appear in the elections toward the end of the decade and the beginning of the 1980s that the Democrats took serious notice. Losing the White House was viewed by some in the Democratic National Committee as a four-year "window" during which the party should rebuild itself. It was then that the major shift to direct mail fund raising and other efforts under the leadership of Chairman Charles Manatt began. The path laid out by the GOP would not immediately fall into place for the Democrats, but they have certainly made great strides toward it.

One point of evidence of the new strength in the national party was the ability of its chairman to survive the efforts of Walter Mondale to unseat him. Manatt's leadership brought him a degree of loyalty from the rest of the party that is rarely seen in Democratic politics. Part of his success was due to the distaste many party leaders felt for the Carter administration in general, and the trouble they saw with Bert Lance, but it also suggests more strength within the organization and is, we believe, a good sign for the future.

Writing, originally in 1977, but copyrighted again in 1978 and 1982, Everett Carll Ladd, a political scientist who publishes frequently in the popular press said of one of the major parties:

> No major party has been so weakly situated vis-a-vis its principal rival as is . . . [this party] today since the death throes of the Federalists in the second decade of the last century. This diminished standing involves more than the fact that the[y] . . . cannot even hope to win control in such arenas as Congress and most state legislatures. [They] have as well experienced such losses among critical elites that it no longer appears as a credible governing party. It is seen by much of informed opinion

in the country as a parochial and reactive alliance, increasingly so, and this alienation of informed opinion constitutes an almost insuperable barrier to the development of an effective alternate public philosophy.[10]

The astute reader will realize he was writing about the Republican party. Informed opinion, notwithstanding, the GOP has proved to be remarkably resilient. The Democrats, however we and they may bemoan their state, are in a stronger position now than the GOP was a few years ago. It still has control of most state governments and the House of Representatives. It has a fighting chance at recapturing the Senate in 1986 and the presidency again in 1988. We do not think it will do as well as it might until it becomes more like the Republicans in professionalism, but neither does anyone seriously believe it will die on the vine. At worst (or best, depending on your partisanship) it will no longer remain the majority party.

DO WE REALLY WANT STRONG PARTIES?

An explanation we often hear for the weakness of the American party system is that it is the best of all possible systems. They are weak because we do not want them to have power. They are weak because we have been vigilant in making certain that power is as widely distributed as possible, as open to public scrutiny as possible, as little used as possible. It has been the nature of our society that promises to each individual the maximum amount of freedom by assuring the least amount of interference. A strong party structure threatens our liberty.

It turns out, however, that a weak party system—at least one as weak as the system under which we lived in the beginning of the second half of the twentieth century—cannot easily cope with strong currents of dissent. It cannot provide focus for political debate, cannot generate commitment to the political system by the public at large. It cannot bring the interests together for compromise and cannot promote consensus.

The turmoil of the 1960s and 1970s came from many different sources: economic changes of a worldwide nature, the search for civil rights, questions of war and peace. The aspirations of the United States in the post-Vietnam era are not as clear as they were after the Second World War. A new generation emerged that seriously questioned the legitimacy of all of the institutions of society, including the parties.

The emergence of volatile interests is a reflection of the weakness of the parties. Were the parties strong, they would be able to contain the interests, or at least to moderate their expectations. We think the parties have begun to do just that as they take the controversial interests of the 1960s and 1970s under their wing. The right and the left have both found greater acceptance in the parties of the 1980s than they did several years ago. It may look as if the parties are being captured by the interests, but we think it is the other way around: the parties are capturing the interests.

The fears of strong parties include a concern that they will freeze out some interests from participation and that their choice of nominees will reflect the status quo; that they will stifle local political expression; that they will use their power unduly to the benefit of their coalition of interests; and that we will not be able to hold them accountable because our choices will be limited to what and whom they choose to offer in each election. There is also an underlying fear that strong parties mean strong government, which in turn may mean an infringement upon our liberty.

The record of strong parties in the past gives substance to the fears. The strongest parties were local machines, eventually brought down because we no longer tolerated their tendency toward corruption and their absolute control of local government. Our memories of strong national parties generally reflect those periods in American history when we faced major crises: the period of the Civil War and reconstruction; the years of the New Deal. In most cases what we recall with displeasure is not so much strong parties as single party domination which allowed dramatic changes if not outright excesses to occur, sometimes to the betterment of society, sometimes not.

A decade and a half ago, David Broder, concluding his book noted that he did not really believe the parties were doomed, not unless we neglect them and the "vital role they can play in re-energizing our political system."[11] But what had passed was the europhia that characterized the nation when he first came to the nation's capital. "Since then, we have gone through the New Frontier and the Great Society and the New American Revolution, each briefer in duration and more patently false in its promise than the slogan that preceded it. If there is one thing the long travail of the last four presidencies has taught us, it is to be skeptical of the easy answer."[12]

We would not suggest that the path is easy, only that it is marked. We do not think strong, professional organizations in Washington will necessarily recreate the faith in ourselves and our institutions we used to have. We do believe in the capacity of these organizations to reach out and build new structures. We believe in the capacity of these organizations to touch the citizenry directly and to recreate in them a commitment to the political system.

The party we have described may seem mechanistic and removed from meaning when compared to our images of older days. To believe that, however, is to miss the nature of the generation that has taken power within the party ranks. They are more diverse than the political bosses who went before: there are many more women, there are more minorities represented. They are also committed to rebuilding the party and are doing so with the tools at hand. To view the growth of professionalism as costing us some intangible quality of democracy is to ignore the reality that more people are more aware that the parties stand for something today.

We believe that the strong national structures we have described are the necessary first step toward political renewal in America. If there is an ebb and flow in these things, we are definitely in the flow as we approach the end of the twentieth century. The prospect is exciting.

David Broder wrote *The Party's Over* in 1971. In the years that followed there were other books by journalist and political scientist alike, decrying the death of the parties. In 1984, Martin P. Wattenberg published a book entitled *The Decline of American Political Parties: 1952–1980,* which may perhaps have been the end of the cycle. Later that year David E. Price, a political scientist who has worked with the Democratic party, published *Bringing Back the Parties.*[13] There may be a new consensus emerging among political scientists who write about the parties. A number have recognized the nationalized nature of the new system, and some have argued that it is becoming federalized, reflecting the structures of government. Theodore J. Lowi has suggested that the parties always reflect the form of government, and it may be that the new party system does reflect a new era in American government. It may take some sorting out to clearly understand how the new party structure relates to a new distribution of power in our government, but it is clear that the party, at least, is going on.

Appendix

The New Law

THE HISTORY of federal campaign finance law goes back to the Progressive Era with the Tillman Act of 1907. It prohibited corporate contributions and was enacted after Theodore Roosevelt's election in which the Republican party raised millions of dollars by systematically assessing corporations around the country. Although this and other laws have been on the books for most of this century at both the national and state levels, loopholes abounded and much of the law was observed more in the breach than in practice.

Beginning again with a Presidential Commission on Campaign Costs following John F. Kennedy's inauguration, initiated in part because the new president was concerned that only a millionaire such as himself could afford to run for office, new life was breathed into the electoral reform effort. Throughout the 1960s, reformers pushed for a new law. The interests that motivated the reformers differed: some were worried about the impact of the media and the amount of money spent in campaigns, some were concerned about the more traditional kinds of abuses of those who give and those who want to raise vast amounts of money.

In 1971, prior to Watergate, Congress passed two bills, the Federal Election Campaign Act (FECA) and the Revenue Act. The latter bill, which provided tax credits or deductions for some political contributions, also provided for the dollar check-off on income tax returns and, consequently, public finance support for the presidential elections. The FECA, which underwent considerable revision in Congress and the courts in the following years, has substantially altered all political activity and, it is our contention, paved the way for the renaissance of the major political parties.

The Federal Election Campaign Act

The FECA passed in 1971 was based on five elements: contributions limits, spending limits, public financing, oversight, and disclosure. Although the components of each of these elements was to change, the basic concept remains, and it has led to a number of changes in the way campaigns at all levels are run.

The 1971 law, due to go into effect in January of 1972, was substantially revised in the 1974 amendments following Watergate. In 1976, when the law was in place, it was again significantly altered with the Supreme Court's ruling in *Buckley* v. *Valeo* in the midst of the presidential campaign. It was amended again in 1979, following the experience of the 1978 elections. Although changes have continued to be discussed and some have passed into law, there have been no major revisions since 1979.

Contribution Limits. The original law in 1971 placed a limit only on the amount a candidate or his family could contribute to a campaign. Ironically, *Buckley* v. *Valeo* did away with that limit and it remains today the only unlimited source of campaign contributions, except for a presidential candidate who receives public funds—and cannot make donations to his own campaign.

The 1974 amendments limited the amount individuals can contribute to campaigns to $1,000 per election and to political action committees ($5,000). PACs can contribute up to $5,000 per election to campaigns. The national political parties are allowed to receive $20,000 from an individual, but there is an aggregate limit of $25,000 that an individual can contribute to all federal elections in any calendar year.

The Supreme Court opened a major exception to the limitations with independent expenditures, whereby an individual or a group can spend as much as he wants, advocating the election or defeat of a candidate, as long as the expenditure is made without any prior communication with the candidate or his or her campaign committee. Basing its opinion on the First Amendment right of free speech and equating money with communication, the Court's initial intention appears to have been to free local groups from the limitations the law imposed, but the vehicle has been used almost exclusively by national single issue and ideological groups.

Spending Limitations. The 1971 law placed a limit on what all federal candidates could spend for media, but both the 1974 amendments and the Court altered the terms. The media provision was revoked and instead the law placed a limit on what presidential candidates who accepted public financing could spend in each state during the primary season (including an aggregate limit nationally, which is less than the sum of the state limits) and during the general election, when the candidate is limited to the amount received from the public treasury. Only one presidential candidate, John Connally, who ran for the Republican nomination in 1980, has thus far chosen not to accept public financing.

Congressional candidates were exempted from the limitations, partly because they were not receiving public funds, and partly because of the politics involved when incumbents write the law under which they will have to run for re-election. The critical issue in congressional limits is how low they could be set because a low limitation favors incumbents. Challengers are invariably less well known and need to spend more money to gain sufficient name recognition to be competitive. Needless to say, there are many other incumbent advantages, a number of which cannot be reasonably quantified.

The parties were also limited in how much they could spend directly on behalf of federal candidates (calculated at 2 cents per voter, which reached up to $20,200 in 1984). In primary elections, the parties are treated as any other nonparty committee and are limited to contributions of $5,000. The national parties are given a limit during the general election period of the presidential campaign ($4.6 million in 1980, $6.9 million in 1984).

Public Financing. Although there has always been discussion of extending public financing to congressional as well as presidential candidates, public funds came into being with the 1974 amendments and are applicable only to presidential elections for candidates of parties. In order to qualify for public financing, a presidential candidate must raise $5,000 in donations of $250 or less in twenty states.

During the primary season, a qualified candidate receives matching funds from the government for each contribution of $250 or less, as long as the candidate wins at least 10 percent of the vote in every primary entered. The two major parties receive flat grants for the nominating conventions (amounting to $8 million each in 1984), and if the party nominee chooses to accept public financing, he is barred from accepting private donations during the general election.

Oversight: The Federal Election Commission. The 1971 law, following the existing tradition, required the Senate and House to police their own elections and the General Accounting Office to oversee the presidential race. The entire structure of oversight was changed in the 1974 amendments with the creation of the Federal Election Commission (FEC), which was to be an independent bipartisan commission of six members chosen by the speaker of the House, the leader of the Senate, and the president. The method of appointment was changed in *Buckley* v. *Valeo,* requiring that all six members be appointed by the president in order to insure the proper separation of the branches of government. The Court notwithstanding, the influence of Congress is still felt quite strongly in commission appointments, which is not surprising given the oversight responsibilities over congressional elections with which the FEC is vested.

The FEC receives and publishes reports on income and expenditures of all federal campaigns, political committees and parties involved in federal campaigns, and individuals and groups who make independent expenditures in federal elections. It also develops the regulations, issues advisory opinions about the law, conducts audits and investigations, issues subpoenas, and has the authority to sue for civil injunctions. Criminal suits are carried out under the aegis of the Justice Department.

Disclosure. If there is one factor in the law above all else that could be said to have altered the nature of American campaigning, it is the requirement that all income and expenditures be disclosed. The reporting requires the centralization and professionalization of campaigns if they are going to comply with the law. It is the disclosure requirement, more than any other provision of the law, which is generally held responsible for the creation and growing importance of campaign legal and accounting professionals and the decrease in decentralized volunteer activity.

The tightening of the campaign structure is burdensome because campaigns are temporary organizations and usually lack the standard operating procedures that make it somewhat easier for more permanent organizations to handle the paperwork involved in compliance. The permanence of the parties, on the other hand, puts them in a better position than most campaigns to respond to the requirements, although the increase in staffing during an election, and the rapid increase of activity as the campaign season reaches its zenith, is burdensome to them as well. At the end of the 1980 election, a presidential campaign year, the RNC reported filing more than 750,000 pages of reports.[1]

In addition to the FECA and the Revenue Act, there were specific pieces of legislation passed in the 1970s that also have had an effect on the parties, the most important of which was the postal subsidy passed in 1978. It permitted the parties to use a rate comparable to the rate available to nonprofit organizations. The effect was to put the costs of direct mail solicitations by the parties on an even basis with the costs of the single issue groups, many of which have nonprofit status because they perform educational services. Given the great dependence of the Republican party, particularly, on direct mail fund raising, the subsidy was an important relief.

The Impact of the Law on the Parties

In 1978, the Campaign Finance Study Group at Harvard did a study for the House Administration Committee on the impact of the campaign finance law.[2] It substantiated what many believed to be true at the time that the law was having an adverse effect on the parties: "A[n] . . . emerging consequence of the campaign act has been a further deterioration of our political parties in the services and resources they can provide to their candidates."[3] This was thought to be particularly true at the local level where grassroots activities had dried up and the national parties had been telling the county and local parties to stay away from federal elections because of the complications of the law, especially the regulations that required a separation of party expenditures (and reporting) for state and federal candidates. Although the law was not originally designed to help the parties directly, the 1979 amendments were intended to at least ameliorate the adverse effects.

As it turned out, however, in later analyses, the law may not have been as responsible for the perceived decline of the grassroots as first thought. In fact, the ability of the parties to provide "services and resources to candidates" was enhanced by the law, if, for no other reason, all other traditional avenues were effectively curtailed.

THE POSITIVE EFFECTS

The argument that the law hurt the parties fell into three categories: the fall-off of grassroots activities, which had been the mainstay of local party participation; the question of services and resources; and the apparent rise of interest groups which seemed to threaten the parties.

The Grassroots Question. We considered the issue of grassroots activities in chapter 2 on party decline and concluded that while it was true that grassroots activities fall off, there were many causes for their decline having more to do with social factors than the law. We also observed, in chapter 4 on state and local parties, that the decline of grassroots activities may turn out to be an incorrect measure of party health because the nature of party organization has changed and is no longer dependent on local activities. Put more specifically, the party is no longer dependent on local volunteers motivated by the material and solidary incentives which maintained local party organizations in years past.

Services and Resources. As to the question of services and resources, it has quite a different answer in the 1980s than it had in the 1970s. Using the Republican party as the prototype, there is no question that the increase in funds during the latter half of the 1970s enabled it to provide a host of services which would have been inconceivable a few years before. It is our belief that if the party were not forced by the law to limit its expenditures directly on behalf of candidates, it would not have devoted as much to "genre" advertising, and the host of noncandidate activities it now engages in.

In addition to the array of activities that the national party has provided its candidates, there are an increasing number of programs not directly linked to specific campaigns. In 1984, some of these programs included special (sometimes controversial) outreach to groups not typically aligned with the GOP, such as Jews and Hispanics, mailings to members of the armed forces overseas who had received absentee ballots, and so on.

Without the financial strength of the national parties, these efforts could not have been undertaken. Who, after all, would have bothered? Each candidate campaign is so bound in to its own uncertainties about victory, its managers cannot afford to appeal to the enemy, Instead, campaign resources are directed partly to known supporters and largely toward marginal supporters who must be kept within the fold. The creative energy it takes to reach out to traditional opponents is a new task that undoubtedly will be added to the repertoire of what parties do—if it proves to be successful.

The capacity to explore new approaches results from the accumulation of new resources. The GOP switch to direct mail fund raising turned out to be rather serendipitous not only because of the money raised but because it turned out to be particularly well suited to the new campaign reporting requirements. The individual donation is small, not likely to exceed contribution limits; and the use of computers to send out the mail and record the returns makes keeping records relatively simple.

The Party and Other Players.   The federal law placed restrictions on every actor and almost every act in the political process. "Fat Cats," although still alive and well in the loopholes of regulation, are no longer dominant in political fund raising. The biggest role they do play (perhaps the biggest loophole), other than independent spending, is with the party. And there are more incentives for large donors to give to the party than to spend it on their own:

- Independent spending requires no contact; large donors give in order to get contact, access.
- Independent spending is not always what the candidate wants.
- Fat Cats usually prefer to keep their efforts moderately private, almost an impossibility with independent spending, but quite possible with donations to the party.
- Many people will give large donations if asked, but will not necessarily volunteer it on their own.
- If donors want to be asked, the party is one of the few actors who can claim close contact with the candidate, but not be limited by the campaign contribution ceiling.

The interest groups have become more institutionalized by the law, which has led some to increase their participation in electoral politics. Although we cannot be sure of the rate of increase because we do not know what happened in the past, it is likely that a corporation that may have given (or encouraged its executives to give) to specific campaigns before, with the creation of a PAC, now gives at every election. But the increased participation does not necessarily mean an increase in money or an increase in influence because PACs are limited in how much they give and are wary about the public nature of it all.

Whether an interest gives more frequently or not, the limits make the party the largest organized donor to any candidate's campaign, directly, and especially indirectly. Because of its capacity to turn out volunteers as well as funds, only labor's participation in the past could challenge the resources of today's political party. But labor's linkage to the Democratic party, while strong, is not likely to be rich enough to help the Democrats balance the activities now undertaken by the GOP. Democratic candidates want the services from their party their Republican opponents get, and labor cannot provide them all, nor is it likely to want to try.

The party's capacity to fill in for the campaign should also not be underestimated. Any volunteer-based activity that a candidate might undertake can be paid for by the party without coming under the spending restrictions. Other exempt expenditures include bumper stickers, campaign paraphenalia, brochures, and so on. Research, including expensive survey analyses, can be paid for by the party and provided to candidates free of charge, or at very reduced rates. The party can pay for media advertising that does not advocate the election or defeat of a specific candidate, but does serve the interests of its own candidates. The party can maintain and provide the lists for fund raising upon which so much depends. It can also provide technological support from the computer programs to the legal advice necessary to sustain a modern campaign. The party can recruit and train candidates and campaign workers (the Democratic party has set up its own school, The Democratic National Training Academy in Des Moines, Iowa). And when it chooses, a party endorsement in primaries carries greater weight than any other interest groups. It can spend thousands of dollars (up to $50,000 in House races) on behalf of its candidates, and millions in presidential elections in which it is the only participant working with the campaign because of the prohibitions against contributing when the election is publicly financed.

In contrast, an individual can donate $1,000 to a campaign and is prohibited from any contribution to a presidential candidate during the general election. A political action committee can contribute up to $5,000 to a candidate. Both individuals and groups can make unrestricted independent expenditures but that avenue, while controversial, has yet to demonstrate a sustaining impact on American politics, especially when there is a great deal of visibility in the race.

The parties have grown more influential under the law because of the restrictions it imposes on the participation of other groups, the limitations it imposes on campaign spending, and on the limitations on contributions from individuals. The law created an opening for the parties, and because of the renewed resources available to the parties, they have been able to take advantage of that opening and are coming to play a more substantial role in elections than any time in recent memory.

Notes

Chapter 1   Introduction

1. David S. Broder, *The Party's Over: The Failure of American Politics* (New York: Harper & Row, 1972).

2. Ibid., p. xi.

3. Jean Blondel, *Political Parties: A Genuine Case for Discontent* (London: Wildhouse, 1978), pp. 12–15.

4. Edmund Burke, *Works,* vol. 1 (London: Routledge & Sons 1865), pp. 525–29.

5. E. E. Schattschneider, *Party Government* (New York: Holt, Rinehart and Winston, 1942), p. 35.

6. Walter Dean Burnham, *Critical Elections and Mainsprings of American Politics* (New York: W. W. Norton, 1970), p. 181.

7. Ibid., p. 183.

8. The story was told at the Presidential Campaign Decision-Makers Conference, 1984, held at the Institute of Politics, John F. Kennedy School of Government, Harvard University, November 30–December 2, 1984.

9. Nelson W. Polsby, *The Consequences of Party Reform* (New York: Oxford University Press, 1983), pp. 132–33.

10. Ibid., p. 133.

11. Ibid.

12. Ibid., pp. 137–38.

13. Ibid., p. 139.

14. Referring to Byron Shafer's argument that it may be due to changes in the elite level, see Byron Shafer, *The Quiet Revolution: The Struggle for the Democratic*

Party and the Shaping of Post-Reform Politics (New York: Russell Sage Foundation, 1984), p. 140.

15. Ibid., p. 141.

16. See Seymour Martin Lipset and William Schneider, *The Confidence Gap: Business, Labor and Government in the Public Mind* (New York: The Free Press, 1983).

Chapter 2   Decline and Fall

1. Norman J. Ornstein, Thomas E. Mann, Michael J. Malbin, and John F. Bibby, *Vital Statistics on Congress, 1982* (Washington, D.C.: American Enterprise Institute, 1982), p. 53.

2. Paul Goodman, "The First Party System," in *The American Party Systems: Stages in Political Development,* ed. William Nisbet Chambers and Walter Dean Burnham, (New York: Oxford University Press, 1967), p. 63.

3. Ibid., pp. 63–64.

4. Ibid.

5. Robert A. Diamond, ed., *Guide to U.S. Elections* (Washington, D.C.: Congressional Quarterly, Inc., 1975), p. 225.

6. Robert H. Wiebe, *The Search for Order: 1877–1920* (New York: Hill & Wang, 1967), p. 27.

7. Joseph Nye, "Corruption and Political Development," *American Political Science Review* 61 (June 1967): 417–27.

8. V. O. Key, Jr., *Politics, Parties and Pressure Groups* (New York: Thomas Y. Crowell, 1942, 1958), pp. 688–89.

9. Austin Ranney, *Curing the Mischiefs of Faction: Party Reform in America* (Berkeley: University of California Press, 1975) p. 81.

10. Ibid.

11. Ibid.; cited originally by Richard Hofstadter, *The Age of Reform* (New York: Vintage Books, 1955), p. 202.

12. Key, *Politics,* p. 411.

13. Ibid., p. 412.

14. Ibid.

15. Ranney, *Mischiefs of Faction,* p. 130.

16. James Sundquist, *Dynamics of the Party System,* rev. ed. (Washington, D.C.: Brookings, 1983), pp. 172–73.

17. Charles R. Adrian, *State and Local Governments,* 4th ed. (New York: McGraw-Hill, 1976), pp. 132–34; and Hugh A. Bone and Austin Ranney, *Politics and Voters* (New York: McGraw-Hill, 1981), p. 68.

18. Ibid.

19. Ibid.

20. *The Kansas City Times,* 18 July 1980.

21. James Q. Wilson, *Political Organizations* (New York: Basic Books, 1973), p. 33.

22. Molly Moore and Michel McQueen, "Legal Expenses Skyrocketing," *The Washington Post,* 13 November 1984, p. A10.

23. A comment made to Xandra Kayden by a University of Massachusetts student when she taught there in the mid–1970s.

24. James Q. Wilson, *The Amateur Democrat* (Chicago: University of Chicago Press, 1962), pp. 3–5.

25. Ibid., p. 165.

26. Ibid., pp. 128–29.

27. Seymour Martin Lipset and William Schneider, *The Confidence Gap: Business, Labor and Government in the Public Mind* (New York: The Free Press, 1983), p. 3.

28. Ibid. pp. 101–7.

29. David S. Broder, *The Party's Over* (New York: Harper & Row, 1972), pp. 247–51.

30. Wilson, *Political Organizations,* p. 34.

31. Ibid., p. 96.

32. See William Schneider, "Half a Realignment," *The New Republic,* 3 December 1984.

Chapter 3   Back from the Depths: Party Resurgence

1. David S. Broder, *The Party's Over: The Failure of American Politics* (New York: Harper & Row, 1972).

2. In 1952, a Democratic national committeeman from Texas chose to support the Republican nominee, Dwight Eisenhower. The DNC refused to seat him and the Texas State Committee went without a representative for three years until it acceded to the national party and named a more acceptable replacement. The opposite situation occurred a few years later in 1958, when the Louisiana Democratic State Committee wanted to unseat its representative to the DNC for being "soft" on civil rights. The national committee refused the state committee the right to determine qualifications for membership to the national body. Both instances were cited in Austin Ranney, *Curing the Mischiefs of Faction: Party Reform in America* (Berkeley: University of California Press, 1975), pp. 27, 101.

3. Byron E. Shafer, *The Quiet Revolution: The Struggle for the Democratic Party and the Shaping of Post-Reform Politics* (New York: Russell Sage Foundation, 1983), pp. 41–43. The issue of balance between reformers and regulars on the commission was critical to both sides. From the perspective of one of the reformers, the full commission was divided equally between reformers and regulars, with 70 percent of the executive committee and 100 percent of the staff drawn from the ranks of the reformers.

From the perspective of the regulars, the division was slightly different: the full executive committee was seen as 64 percent reformer to 36 percent regular; the executive committee as 80 percent reform and the staff as 100 percent reform. Either way, the tilt toward the reformers had a significant impact on the party during the following decade. It was the battle line within the party until at least 1980. (Drawn from analyses by Eli Segal, a reformer, and Al Barkan, director of COPE, AFL–CIO, a representative of the regulars. Shafer, *The Quiet Revolution,* pp. 85, 95.

4. Drawn from Austin Ranney, Byron E. Shafer, Nelson Polsby, and Aaron Wildavsky, *Presidential Elections: Strategies of American Electoral Politics,* 4th ed. (New York: Charles Scribner's Sons, 1976).

5. Carol F. Casey, "The National Democratic Party," in *Party Renewal in America: Theory and Practice,* ed. Gerald M. Pomper, (New York: Praeger, 1981), p. 91.

6. Charles T. Manatt, Chairman of the Democratic National Committee, "Charge to the Commission on Presidential Nomination," mimeo, 2 July 1981.

7. Patrick Caddell, unpublished memorandum, 5 February 1982, p. 2.

8. Memorandum from Rick Stearns, Technical Advisory Committee, to the Hunt Commission, re: Rules Reflections, undated.

9. Shafer, *The Quiet Revolution* p. 7.

10. See David S. Broder, *The Changing of the Guard: Power and Leadership in*

America (New York: Penguin Books, 1980); and Xandra Kayden, *Campaign Organization* (Lexington, Mass.: D.C. Heath, 1978).

11. Interview with Wyatt Stewart, Finance Director of the Republican Congressional Committee, 14 November 1984.

12. Ibid.

13. "FEC Reports Republicans Outspent Democrats by More than 5-to-1 in '82 Elections," Press Release from the Federal Election Commission, 26 April 1983.

14. Martin Schram, *The Washington Post,* 21 March 1982, p. A-2.

15. The FEC turned back a bid by Representative Tony Coelho in 1984, which argued that the advertising represented a campaign contribution and should be counted under the party contribution limitations.

16. "Chairman's Report," Republican National Committee, Washington, D.C., 1980, p. 2.

17. "Chairman's Report," Republican National Committee, Washington, D.C., 1979, p. 23.

18. Ibid.

19. Ibid.

20. "Chairman's Report," Republican National Committee, Washington, D.C., 1982, p. 32.

21. Ibid.

22. "Chairman's Report," Republican National Committee, Washington, D.C., 1981, p. 16.

23. Sabato, *The Rise of Political Consultants,* pp. 330–31.

24. FEC Report, cited in *The Sunday Globe,* 4 November 1984.

25. Ibid.

26. David Adamany, "Political Parties in the 1980 Election," in *Money and Politics in the United States: Financing Elections in the 1980s,* ed. Michael S. Malbin (Chatham, N.J.: Chatham Press and the American Enterprise Institute, 1984).

27. Cornelius P. Cotter and John F. Bibby, "Institutional Development of Parties and the Thesis of Party Decline," *Political Science Quarterly* 95 (Spring, 1980).

28. Morton Kondracke, "CPR for Political Parties," *The Washington Times,* 22 October 1984.

Chapter 4   The Grassroots No Longer Count But the State
Party Lives On

1. Cited in "An Analysis of the Impact of the Federal Election Campaign Act 1972–78," Campaign Finance Study Group, Institute of Politics, Harvard University, 1978, p. 96.

2. Ruth S. Jones, "State Election Campaign Financing: 1980," in *Money and Politics in the United States: Financing Elections in the 1980s,* ed. Michael J. Malbin (Chatham, N.J.: Chatham Press and the American Enterprise Institute, 1984).

3. Ibid.

4. Ibid.

5. Reported in Xandra Kayden, "Parties and the 1980 Presidential Election," in "Financing Presidential Campaigns," the Campaign Finance Study Group, Institute of Politics, Harvard University, 1982, pp. 6, 16–17.

6. Interview in Washington, D.C., with Xandra Kayden, August 1983.

7. Xandra Kayden, "Parties and the 1980 Presidential Election."

8. Ibid., pp. 6, 20–21.

9. Nelson W. Polsby, *Consequences of Party Reform* (New York: Oxford University Press, 1983), pp. 141–42.

10. Flyer from the Republican National Committee, 1980.
11. John H. Aldrich, *Before the Convention: Strategies and Choices in Presidential Nomination Campaigns* (Chicago: University of Chicago Press, 1980), p. 8.
12. Dennis Farney, "Rep. Coelho Makes Money, and Waves, for the Democrats: Chief of Campaign Committee Stirs Unease by Seeking Business Contributors," *The Wall Street Journal*, 14 June 1983.

Chapter 5 Why the Interest Groups Can't Beat the Parties

1. Elizabeth Drew, *Politics and Money: The New Road to Corruption* (New York: Macmillan, 1983).
2. F. Christopher Arterton, "Dollars for Presidents: Spending Money Under the FECA," in "Financing Presidential Campaigns: An Examination of the Ongoing Effects of the Federal Election Campaigns Laws upon the Conduct of Presidential Campaigns," by the Campaign Finance Study Group to the Committee on Rules and Administration of the United States Senate (Cambridge: Institute of Politics, Harvard University, 1982), pp. 3–4, 5.
3. John Milne, "PAC Funds Playing Large Role in N.H. Senate campaign," *Boston Sunday Globe*, 30 September 1984, p. 62.
4. Michael J. Malbin, "Looking Back at the Future of Campaign Finance Reform: Interest Groups and American Elections," in *Money and Politics in the United States*, ed. Michael Malbin (Chatham, N.J.: Chatham and the American Enterprise Institute, 1984).
5. The statistics cited and the case itself are reported in Xandra Kayden, "The Nationalizing of the Party System," in *Parties, Interest Groups and Campaign Finance Laws*, ed. Michael J. Malbin, (Washington, D.C.: American Enterprise Institute, 1979), pp. 270–75.
6. Ibid.
7. Ibid., p. 275.
8. Press release from the Federal Election Commission, 26 October 1984.
9. Drawn from FEC data, reported by Xandra Kayden, "Independent Spending," in "Financing Presidential Campaigns: An Examination of the Ongoing Effects of the Federal Election Campaign Laws upon the Conduct of Presidential Campaigns," by the Campaign Finance Study Group for the Committee on Rules and Administration of the United States Senate (Cambridge: Institute of Politics, Harvard University, January, 1982) and in Xandra Kayden, "Campaign Finance and the Presidential Selection Process," in Alexander Heard and Michael Nelson, eds., *The Presidential Selection Process* (forthcoming).
10. Xandra Kayden studied the re-election campaign of Senator Birch Bayh in Indiana in 1980 and found some evidence that it made a difference: "On the Sunday before the election, the polls showed the candidate in a dead heat: forty-one percent for each; forty-four percent each if the 'leaners' among the undecided were included. Bayh had come back in the polls, so there was a possibility the momentum would carry him to victory. The election, however, was not a close one. The activities of the Moral Majority throughout that last weekend may have made the difference. Sermons, telephone and door-to-door canvassing of church members, and leafleting [paid for by independent spending groups and individuals] probably had some effect. . . . The argument can be made, but it cannot be proved." in Xandra Kayden, "Campaign Under Siege: Reflections on One Senator's Defeat," in *New York University Review of Law and Social Change* X, no. 1 (1980–81): 77.
11. *Boston Sunday Globe*, 30 September 1984, p. 43.
12. John T. Dolan, reported in *The Washington Post*, 10 August 1980.

13. Cited in Xandra Kayden, "Independent Spending," Campaign Finance Study Group Study, 1982, p. 7–12.

14. James Madison, "The Federalist Paper No. 10," *The Federalist Papers,* ed. Roy P. Fairchild, 2nd ed., (New York: Doubleday Anchor Books, 1966), p. 17.

15. E. E. Schattschneider, *The Semi-Sovereign People* (New York: Holt, Rinehart and Winston, 1960), pp. 2–4.

16. Comments made at the Presidential Campaign Decision-Makers Conference, 1984, Institute of Politics, John F. Kennedy School of Government, Harvard University, November 30–December 2, 1984.

17. Ibid.

18. Schattschneider, *The Semi-Sovereign People,* p. 59.

Chapter 6   That Elusive Arbiter: The Voter

1. *Boston Globe,* 18 November 1984.

2. Norman H. Nie, Sidney Verba, and John R. Petrocik, *The Changing American Voter,* enlarged ed. (Harvard University Press, 1976, 1979), pp. 44–46; Angus Campbell, Philip E. Converse, Warren E. Miller, and Donald E. Stokes, *The American Voter* (New York: John Wiley & Sons, 1964).

3. Nie, Verba, and Petrocik, *The Changing American Voter,* p. 46.

4. Telephone interview with Wyatt Stewart, 14 November 1984.

5. Philip E. Converse and Gregory B. Markus, "Plus ça change . . . : The New CPS Election Panel," *American Political Science Review* 73, no. 1 (March 1979): 36.

6. "*The New York Times*/CBS News Poll," *New York Times,* 8 November 1984., p. A19.

7. Seymour Martin Lipset and William Schneider, *The Confidence Gap* (New York: The Free Press, 1983), pp. 101–4.

8. Ibid., pp. 104–5. Included in the twelve institutions are business, labor, government, etc.

9. V. O. Key, Jr., *Southern Politics in State and Nation* (New York: Alfred A. Knopf, 1950).

10. Alan Baron, "The Baron Report," no. 218, (19 November 1984), p. 2.

11. "The *New York Times*/CBS Poll," *New York Times,* 18 November 1984, p. A19.

12. Ibid.

13. Cited from data adopted from the Center for Political Studies, University of Michigan and Nie, Verba, and Petrocik in David E. Price, *Bringing Back the Parties* (CQ Press, 1974), p. 15.

14. William Schneider, "Half a Realignment," *The New Republic,* 3 December 1984, p. 22.

15. "*New York Times*/CBS Poll."

16. Schneider, "Half a Realignment."

17. Alan Baron, "The Baron Report," 18 June 1984.

18. Ibid.

19. Presidential Campaign Decision-Makers Conference, 1984, Institute of Politics, John F. Kennedy School of Government, Harvard University, November 30–December 2, 1984.

20. *Boston Globe,* 12 November 1984.

21. Ibid.

22. Presidential Campaign Decision-Makers Conference.

23. Drawn from data collected by John F. Bibby, Thomas E. Mann, and Norman J. Ornstein, *Vital Statistics on Congress, 1980* (Washington, D. C.: American Enter-

prise Institute, 1980); and Martin P. Wattenberg, *The Decline of American Political Parties: 1952–1980 (Cambridge: Harvard University Press, 1984)*, p. 19.
24. Warren E. Miller and Therese E. Levitan, *Leadership and Change: The New Politics and the American Electorate* (Englewood, N.J.: Winthrop, 1976).
25. Harris Survey, *Boston Globe*, 11 November 1984.
26. Ibid.

Chapter 7   The New Party System

1. David S. Broder, *The Party's Over: The Failure of American Politics* (New York: Harper & Row, 1972), p. 254.
2. Ibid., pp. 255–56.
3. See chapter 4 herein.
4. Presidential Campaign Decision-Makers Conference, 1984, Institute of Politics, John F. Kennedy School of Government, Harvard University, November 30–December 2, 1984.
5. David S. Broder, *The Changing of the Guard* (New York: Simon and Shuster, 1980); Xandra Kayden, *Campaign Organization* (Lexington, Mass.: D. C. Heath, 1978).
6. Broder, *The Changing of the Guard*, p. 1.
7. David Nyan, "The GOP Fund Raisers Sound the Alarm," *The Sunday Globe*, 21 October 1984; "Helms-Hunt Contest: $25m," *Boston Globe*, 10 December 1984.
8. "Helms-Hunt Contest: $25m," *Boston Globe*.
9. Cornelius P. Cotter and John F. Bibby, "Institutional Development of Parties and the Thesis of Party Decline," *Political Science Quarterly* 95 (Spring 1980).
10. Everett Carll Ladd, *Where Have All the Voters Gone: The Fracturing of America's Political Parties*, 2nd ed. (New York: W. W. Norton & Co., 1982), p. *xxvi.*
11. Broder, *The Party's Over*, p. 264.
12. Ibid.
13. Martin P. Wattenberg, *The Decline of American Political Parties: 1952–1980* (Cambridge: Harvard University Press, 1984); David E. Price, *Bringing Back the Parties* (Washington, D.C.: Congressional Quarterly Press, 1984).

Appendix   The New Law

1. Interview conducted by Xandra Kayden in Washington, D.C., 13 October 1981; reported in "Financing Presidential Campaigns," Campaign Finance Study Group, pp. 6–23; "Chairman's Report," Republican National Committee, Washington, D.C., 1981, p. 15.
2. "An Analysis of the Impact of the Federal Election Campaign Act, 1972–78," from the Institute of Politics, John F. Kennedy School of Government, Harvard University, prepared for the Committee on House Administration of the U.S. House of Representatives (Washington D.C.: U.S. Government Printing Office, 1979).
3. Ibid., p. 2.

INDEX